SERMONS OF
ROBERT MURRAY M'CHEYNE

SERMONS OF
ROBERT MURRAY M'CHEYNE

THE BANNER OF TRUTH TRUST

THE BANNER OF TRUTH TRUST
3 Murrayfield Road, Edinburgh EH12 6EL
P.O. Box 621, Carlisle, Pennsylvania 17013, U.S.A.

*

This selection from R. M. M'Cheyne's
sermons first published 1961
Reprinted 1972
Reprinted 1985
Reprinted 1986

ISBN 0 85151 165 1

*

Set in 11 on 12 point Modern
and printed by McCorquodale (Scotland) Ltd.

PUBLISHER'S FOREWORD

FEW of M'Cheyne's sermons were published during his lifetime. After his death at the age of twenty-nine, in 1843, his friend Andrew Bonar published the well-known volume, *Memoir and Remains of R. M. M'Cheyne*. It is less generally known that two further volumes subsequently appeared and it is from these that the following sermons (except the final one, which was published in a pamphlet entitled *Two Last Discourses*, 1843) have been selected. Sermons 1 to 17 are from *Additional Remains of R. M. M'Cheyne*, 1846; it should be borne in mind that they were not prepared by the author for publication being his MS. notes which he generally expanded in delivering. Sermons 18 to 25 are from *A Basket of Fragments*, 1848, the contents of which did not originate from the author's MSS. but from the notes of his hearers, taken down during the course of his ministry " without the least view to publication." Although it has this disadvantage, " yet," as the editor of the first edition wrote, " it brings before us those extemporaneous pleadings with sinners in which few so greatly excelled. He lived and laboured for the conversion of souls. This end, we trust, may, in some measure, be accomplished by the publication of these Sermons, many through them being turned from darkness unto light and from the power of sin and Satan unto God."

CONTENTS

THE LOVE OF CHRIST

" For the love of Christ constraineth us; because we thus judge, that if
one died for all, then were all dead."—2 Cor. v. 14.

OF all the features of St. Paul's character, untiring activity was
the most striking. From his early history, which tells us of his
personal exertions in wasting the infant Church, when he was a
" blasphemer, and a persecutor, and injurious," it is quite obvious
that this was the prominent characteristic of his natural mind. But
when it pleased the Lord Jesus Christ to show forth in him all long
suffering, and to make him " a pattern to them which should afterwards believe on Him," it is beautiful and most instructive to see
how the natural features of this daringly bad man became not only
sanctified, but invigorated and enlarged; so true it is that they that
are in Christ are a new creation. Old things pass away, and all things
become new. " *Troubled* on every side, yet not distressed; *per-
plexed*, but not in despair; *persecuted*, but not forsaken; *cast down*,
but not destroyed "—this was a faithful picture of the life of the
converted Paul. Knowing the terror of the Lord, and the
fearful situation of all who were yet in their sins, he made it the
business of his life to persuade men—striving if, by any means,
he might commend the truth to their consciences. " For (saith he)
whether we be beside ourselves, it is to God; or whether we be sober,
it is for your cause." (Verse 13.) Whether the world think us wise
or mad, the cause of God and of human souls is the cause in which we
have embarked all the energies of our being. Who, then, is not
ready to inquire into the secret spring of all these supernatural
labours ? Who would not desire to have heard from the lips of
Paul what mighty principle it was that impelled him through so
many toils and dangers ? What magic spell has taken possession of
this mighty mind, or what unseen planetary influence, with unceasing

1

power, draws him on through all discouragements—indifferent alike to the world's dread laugh, and the fear of man, which bringeth a snare—careless alike of the sneer of the sceptical Athenian, of the frown of the luxurious Corinthian, and the rage of the narrow-minded Jew ? What saith the apostle himself ? for we have his own explanation of the mystery in the words before us: " *The love of Christ constraineth us.*"

That Christ's love to man is here intended, and not our love to the Saviour, is quite obvious, from the explanation which follows, where his dying for all is pointed to as the instance of his love. It was the view of that strange compassion of the Saviour, moving him to die for his enemies—to bear double for all our sins—to taste death for every man—it was this view which gave him the impulse in every labour—which made all suffering light to him, and every commandment not grievous. He "ran with patience the race that was set·before him." Why ? Because, "looking unto Jesus," he lived a man " crucified unto the world, and the world crucified unto him." By what means ? By looking to the cross of Christ. As the natural sun in the heavens exercises a mighty and unceasing attractive energy on the planets which circle round it, so did the Sun of Righteousness, which had indeed arisen on Paul with a brightness above that of noon-day, exercise on his mind a continual and an almighty energy, *constraining* him to live henceforth no more unto himself, but to him that died for him and rose again. And observe, that it was no temporary, fitful energy, which it exerted over his heart and life, but an abiding and a continued attraction; for he doth not say that the love of Christ *did once* constrain him; or that it *shall yet* constrain him; or that in times of excitement, in seasons of prayer, or peculiar devotion, the love of Christ *was wont* to constrain him; but he saith simply, that the love of Christ *constraineth* him. It is the ever-present, ever-abiding, ever-moving power, which forms the main-spring of all his working; so that, take that away, and his energies are gone, and Paul is become weak as other men.

Is there no one before me whose heart is longing to possess just such a master-principle ? Is there no one of you, brethren, who has

2

arrived at that most interesting of all the stages of salvation in which you are panting after a power to make you new ? You have entered in at the strait gate of believing. You have seen that there is no peace to the unjustified; and therefore you have put on Christ for your righteousness; and already you feel something of the joy and peace of believing. You can look back on your past life, spent without God in the world, and without Christ in the world, and without the Spirit in the world—you can see yourself a condemned outcast, and you say: "Though I should wash my hands in snow-water, yet mine own clothes would abhor me." You can do all this, with shame and self-reproach it is true, but yet without dismay, and without despair; for your eye has been lifted believingly to him who was made sin for us, and you are persuaded that, as it pleased God to count all your iniquities to the Saviour, so he is willing, and hath always been willing, to count all the Saviour's righteousness to you. Without despair, did I say ? nay, with joy and singing; for if, indeed, thou believest with all thine heart, then thou art come to the blessedness of the man unto whom God imputeth righteousness without works—which David describes, saying: "Blessed are they whose iniquities are forgiven, and whose sins are covered. Blessed is the man to whom the Lord imputeth not sin." This is the peace of the justified man. But is this peace a state of perfect blessedness ? Is there nothing left to be desired ? I appeal to those of you who know what it is to be just by believing. What is it that still clouds the brow—that represses the exulting of the spirit ? Why might we not always join in the song of thanksgiving, "Bless the Lord, O my soul, and forget not all his benefits: who forgiveth all thine iniquities"? If we have received double for all our sins, why should it ever be needful for us to argue as doth the Psalmist: "Why art thou cast down, O my soul; and why art thou disquieted in me ? " Ah ! my friends, there is not a man among you, who has really believed, who has not felt the disquieting thought of which I am now speaking. There may be some of you who have felt it so painfully, that it has obscured, as with a heavy cloud, the sweet light of Gospel peace—the shining in of the reconciled countenance upon the soul. The thought is this, " I am a justified man; but, alas ! I am not a

3

sanctified man. I can look at my past life without despair; but how can I look forward to what is to come?"

There is not a more picturesque moral landscape in the universe than such a soul presents. Forgiven all trespasses that are past, the eye looks inwards with a clearness and an impartiality unknown before, and there it gazes upon its long-fostered affections for sin, which like ancient rivers, have worn a deep channel into the heart— its periodic returns of passion, hitherto irresistible and overwhelming, like the tides of the ocean—its perversities of temper and of habit, crooked and unyielding, like the gnarled branches of a stunted oak. Ah! what a scene is here—what anticipations of the future! what forebodings of a vain struggle against the tyranny of lust!— against old trains of acting, and of speaking, and of thinking! Were it not that the hope of the glory of God is one of the chartered rights of the justified man, who would be surprised if this view of terror were to drive a man back, like the dog to his vomit, or the sow that was washed to wallow again in the mire? Now it is to the man precisely in this situation, crying out at morning and at evening, How shall I be made new?—what good shall the forgiveness of my past sins do me, if I be not delivered from the love of sin?— it is to that man that we would now, with all earnestness and affec- tion, point out the example of Paul, and the secret power which wrought in him. " *The love of Christ* (says Paul) *constraineth us.*" We, too, are men of like passions with yourselves: that same sight which you view with dismay within you, was in like manner revealed to us in all its discouraging power. Nay, ever and anon the same hideous view of our own hearts is opened up to us. But we have an encouragement which never fails. The love of the bleeding Saviour constraineth us. The Spirit is given to them that believe; and that almighty Agent hath one argument that moves us continually—THE LOVE OF CHRIST.

My present object, brethren, is to show *how* this argument, in the hand of the Spirit, does move the believer to live unto God— how so simple a truth as the love of Christ to man, continually presented to the mind by the Holy Ghost, should enable any man to live a life of Gospel holiness; and if there be one man among you

4

whose great inquiry is, How shall I be saved from sin—how shall I walk as a child of God?—that is the man, of all others, whose ear and heart I am anxious to engage.

1. *The love of Christ to man constraineth the believer to live a holy life, because that truth takes away all his dread and hatred of God.* When Adam was unfallen, God was everything to his soul; and everything was good and desirable to him, only in so far as it had to do with God. Every vein of his body, so fearfully and wonderfully made—every leaf that rustled in the bowers of Paradise—every new sun that rose, rejoicing like a strong man to run his race—brought him in every day new subjects of godly thought and of admiring praise; and it was only for that reason that he could delight to look on them. The flowers that appeared on the earth—the singing of birds, and the voice of the turtle heard throughout the happy land—the fig tree putting forth her green figs, and the vines with the tender grapes giving a good smell—all these combined to bring in to him *at every pore* a rich and varied tribute of pleasantness. And why? Just because they brought into the soul rich and varied communications of the manifold grace of Jehovah. For, just as you may have seen a child on earth devoted to its earthly parent—pleased with everything when he is present, and valuing every gift just as it shows more of the tenderness of that parent's heart—so was it with that genuine child of God. In God he lived, and moved, and had his being; and not more surely would the blotting out the sun in the heavens have taken away that light which is so pleasant to the eyes, than would the hiding of the face of God from him have taken away the light of his soul, and left nature a dark and desolate wilderness. But when Adam fell, the fine gold became dim—the system of his thoughts and likings was just reversed. Instead of enjoying God in everything, and everything in God, everything now seemed hateful and disagreeable to him, just in as far as it had to do with God.

When man sinned, he began to fear God and also to hate him; and fled to all sin, just to flee from Him whom he hated. So that, just as you may have seen a child who has grievously transgressed against a loving parent, doing all it can to hide from that

5

parent—hurrying from his presence, and plunging into other thoughts and occupations, just to rid itself of the thought of its justly offended father—in the very same way when fallen Adam heard the voice of the Lord God walking in the garden in the cool of the day—that voice which, before he sinned, was heavenly music in his ears—*then did Adam and his wife hide themselves from the presence of the Lord, among the trees of the garden.* And in the same way does every natural man run from the voice and presence of the Lord—not to hide under the thick embowering leaves of Paradise, but to bury himself in cares, and business, and pleasures, and revellings. Any retreat is agreeable, where God is not—any occupation is tolerable, if God be not in the thoughts. Now I am quite sure that many of you may hear this charge against the natural man with incredulous indifference, if not with indignation. You do not feel that you hate God, or dread his presence; and, therefore, you say it cannot be true. But, brethren, when God says of your heart that it is " desperately wicked," yea, unsearchably wicked— who can know it ?—when God claims for himself the privilege of knowing and trying the heart—is it not presumptuous in such ignorant beings as we are, to say that that is not true, with respect to our hearts, which God affirms to be true, merely because we are not conscious of it ? God saith that "*the carnal mind is enmity against God* "—that the very grain and substance of an unconverted mind is hatred against God—absolute, implacable hatred against Him in whom we live, and move, and have our being. It is quite true that we do not feel this hatred within us; but that is only an aggravation of our sin and of our danger. We have so choked up the avenues of self-examination—there are so many turnings and windings, before we can arrive at the true motives of our actions— that our dread and hatred of God, which first moved man to sin, and which are still the grand impelling forces whereby Satan goads on the children of disobedience—these are wholly concealed from our view, and you cannot persuade a natural man that they are really there. But the Bible testifies, that out of these two deadly roots— dread of God and hatred of God—grows up the thick forest of sins with which the earth is blackened and overspread. And if there

6

be one among you, brethren, who has been awakened by God to know what is in his heart, I take that man this day to witness, that his bitter cry, in the view of all his sins, has ever been: " *Against thee, thee only*, have I sinned."

If, then, dread of God, and hatred of God, be the cause of all our sins, how shall we be cured of the love of sin, but by taking away the cause ? How do you most effectually kill the noxious weed ? is it not by striking at the root ? In the love of Christ to man, then—in that strange unspeakable gift of God, when he laid down his life for his enemies—when he died the just for the unjust, that he might bring us to God—do not you see an object which, if really believed by the sinner, takes away all his dread and all his hatred of God ? The root of sin is severed from the stock. In His bearing double for all our sins, we see the curse carried away—we see God reconciled. Why should we fear any more ? Not fearing, why should we hate God any more ? Not hating God, what desirableness can we see in sin any more ? Putting on the righteousness of Christ, we are again placed as Adam was—*with God* as our friend. We have no object in sinning; and, therefore, we do not care to sin. In the 6th chapter of Romans, Paul seems to speak of the believer sinning, as if the very proposition was absurd: " How shall we that are dead to sin "—that is, who in Christ have already borne the penalty—" how shall we live any longer therein ? " And again he saith very boldly: " Sin *shall not* have dominion over you "—it is impossible in the nature of things—" for ye are not under the law, but under grace "— ye are no longer under the curse of a broken law, dreading and hating God; ye are under grace—under a system of peace and friendship with God.

But is there anyone ready to object to me, that if these things be so—if nothing more than that a man be brought into peace with God is needful to a holy life and conversation—how comes it that believers do still sin ? I answer, It is indeed too true that believers do sin; but it is just as true that unbelief is the cause of their sinning. If, brethren, you and I were to live with our eye so closely on Christ bearing double for all our sins—freely offering to all a double righteousness for all our sins; and if this constant view of the love of

Christ maintained within us—as assuredly it would, if we looked with a straightforward eye—the peace of God which passeth all understanding—the peace that rests on nothing in us, but upon the completeness that is in Christ—then, brethren, I do say, that frail and helpless as we are, we should never sin—we should not have the slightest object in sinning. But, ah! my friends, this is not the way with us. How often in the day is the love of Christ quite out of view! How often is it obscured to us!—sometimes hid from us by God himself, to teach us what we are. How often are we left without the realizing sense of the completeness of his offering—the perfectness of his righteousness, and without the will or the confidence to claim an interest in him! Who can wonder, then, that, where there is so much unbelief, dread and hatred of God should again and again creep in, and sin should often display its poisonous head? The matter is very plain, brethren, if only we had spiritual eyes to see it. If we live a life of faith on the Son of God, then we shall assuredly live a life of holiness. I do not say, *we ought to do so*; but I say we shall, as a matter of necessary consequence. But, in as far as we do not live a life of faith, in so far we shall live a life of unholiness. It is through faith that God purifies the heart; and there is no other way.

Is there any of you, then, brethren, desirous of being made new—of being delivered from the slavery of sinful habits and affections? We can point you to no other remedy than the love of Christ. Behold how he loved you! See what he bore for you—put your finger, as it were, into the prints of the nails, and thrust your hand into his side; and be no more faithless, but believing. Under a sense of your sins, flee to the Saviour of sinners. As the timorous dove flies to hide itself in the crevices of the rock, so do you flee to hide yourself in the wounds of your Saviour; and when you have found him like the shadow of a great rock in a weary land—when you sit under his shadow with great delight—you will find that he hath slain all the enmity—that he hath accomplished all your warfare. God is now for you. Planted together with Christ in the likeness of his death, you shall be also in the likeness of his resurrection. Dead unto sin, you shall be alive unto God.

2. *The love of Christ to man constraineth the believer to live a holy life, because that truth not only takes away our fear and hatred, but stirs up our love.* When we are brought to see the reconciled face of God in peace—that is a great privilege. But how can we look upon that face, reconciling and reconciled, and not love him who hath so loved us ? Love begets love. We can hardly keep from esteeming those on earth who really love us, however worthless they may be. But, ah ! my friends, when we are convinced that God loves us, and convinced in such a way as by the giving up of his Son for us all, how can we but love him in whom are all excellences—everything to call forth love? I have already shown you that the Gospel is a restorative scheme; it brings us back to the same state of friendship with God which Adam enjoyed, and thus takes away the desire of sin. But now I wish to show you that the Gospel does far more than restore us to the state from which we fell. If rightly and consistently embraced by us, it brings us into a state far better than Adam's. It constrains us by a far more powerful motive. Adam had not this strong love of God to man shed abroad in his heart; and, therefore, he had not this constraining power to make him live to God. But our eyes have seen this great sight. Before us Christ hath been evidently set forth crucified. If we have truly believed, his love hath brought us into peace, through pardon; and because we are pardoned and at peace with God, the Holy Ghost is given us. What to do ? Why, just to shed abroad this truth over our hearts—to show us more and more of this love of God to us, that we may be drawn to love him who hath so loved us—to live to him who died for us and rose again.

It is truly admirable, to see how the Bible way of making us holy is suited to our nature. Had God proposed to frighten us into a holy life, how vain would have been the attempt ! Men have always an idea, that if one came from the dead to tell us of the reality of the doleful regions where dwell, in endless misery, the spirits of the damned, that that would constrain us to live a holy life; but, alas ! brethren, what ignorance does this show of our mysterious nature ! Suppose that God should this hour unveil before our eyes the secrets of those dreadful abodes where hope never comes; nay,

9

suppose, if it were possible, that you were actually made to feel for a season the real pains of the lake of living agony, and the worm that never dies; and then that you were brought back again to the earth, and placed in your old situation, among your old friends and companions; do you really think that there would be any chance of your walking as a child with God ?   I doubt not you would be frightened out of your positive sins; the cup of godless pleasure would drop from your hand—you would shudder at an oath—you would tremble at a falsehood; because you had seen and felt something of the torment which awaits the drunkard, and the swearer, and the liar, in the world beyond the grave; but do you really think that you would live to God any more than you did—that you would serve him better than before ?   It is quite true you might be driven to give larger charity; yea, to give all your goods to feed the poor, and your body to be burned; you might live strictly and soberly, most fearful of breaking one of the commandments, all the rest of your days; but this would not be living to God; you would not love him one whit more.   Ah ! brethren, you are sadly blinded to your curiously formed hearts, if you do not know that love cannot be forced; no man was ever frightened into love, and, therefore, no man was ever frightened into holiness.

But thrice blessed be God, he hath invented a way more powerful than hell and all its terrors—an argument mightier far than even a sight of those torments—he hath invented a way of *drawing us* to holiness.   By showing us the love of his Son, he calleth forth our love.   He knew our frame—he remembered that we were dust—he knew all the peculiarities of our treacherous hearts; and, therefore, he suited his way of sanctifying to the creature to be sanctified. And thus, the Spirit doth not make use of terror to sanctify us, but of love: " *The love of Christ constraineth us.*"   *He draws us by* " *the cords of love—by the bands of a man.*"   What parent does not know that the true way to gain the obedience of a child, is to gain the affections of the child ?   And think you God, who gave us this wisdom, doth not himself know it ?   Think you he would set about obtaining the obedience of his children, without first of all gaining their affections ?   To gain our affections, brethren, which by nature

10

rove over the face of the earth, and centre anywhere but in him, God hath sent his Son into the world to bear the curse of our sins. "Though he was rich, yet for our sakes he became poor, that we, through his poverty, might be made rich."

And, oh ! if there is but one of you who will consent this day, under a sense of undoneness, to flee for refuge to the Saviour, to find in him the forgiveness of all sins that are past, I know well, that from this day forth you will be like that poor woman which was a sinner, which stood at Christ's feet behind him, weeping, and began to wash his feet with tears, and did wipe them with the hairs of her head; and kissed his feet, and anointed them with the ointment. Forgiven much, you will love much—loving much, you will live to the service of Him whom you love. This is the grand master-principle of which we spoke; this is the secret spring of all the holiness of the saints. The life of holiness is not what the world falsely represents it—a life of preciseness and painfulness, in which a man crosses every affection of his nature. There is no such thing as self-denial, in the Popish sense of that word, in the religion of the Bible. The system of restrictions and self-crossings, is the very system which Satan hath set up as a counterfeit of God's way of sanctifying. It is thus that Satan frightens away thousands from Gospel peace and Gospel holiness; as if to be a sanctified man were to be a man who crossed every desire of his being—who did everything that was disagreeable and uncomfortable to him. My friends, our text distinctly shows you that it is not so. We are constrained to holiness by the love of Christ; the love of him who loved us, is the only cord by which we are bound to the service of God. The scourge of our affections is the only scourge that drives us to duty. Sweet bands, and gentle scourges ! Who would not be under their power ?

And, finally, brethren, if Christ's love to us be the object which the Holy Ghost makes use of, at the very first, to draw us to the service of Christ, it is by means of the same object that he draws us onwards, to persevere even unto the end. So that if you are visited with seasons of coldness and indifference—if you begin to be weary, or lag behind in the service of God, behold ! here is the remedy: Look again to the bleeding Saviour. That Sun of Righteousness

11

is the grand attractive centre, round which all his saints move swiftly, and in smooth harmonious concert—"*not without song.*" As long as the believing eye is fixed upon his love, the path of the believer is easy and unimpeded; for that love always constraineth. But lift off the believing eye, and the path becomes impracticable— the life of holiness a weariness.   Whosoever, then, would live a life of persevering holiness, let him keep his eye fixed on the Saviour.   As long as Peter looked only to the Saviour, he walked upon the sea in safety, to go to Jesus; but when he looked around, and saw the wind boisterous, he was afraid, and, beginning to sink, cried, " Lord, save me ! "   Just so will it be with you.   As long as you look believingly to the Saviour, who loved you and gave himself for you, so long you may tread the waters of life's troubled sea, and the soles of your feet shall not be wet; but venture to look around upon the winds and waves that threaten you on every hand, and, like Peter, you begin to sink, and cry, " Lord, save me ! "   How justly, then, may we address to you the Saviour's rebuke to Peter: " O thou of little faith, wherefore didst thou doubt ? "   Look again to the love of the Saviour, and behold that love which constraineth thee to live no more to thyself, but to him that died for thee and rose again.

College Church, Aug. 30, 1835.

A TIME OF REFRESHING

" For I will pour water upon him that is thirsty, and floods upon the dry ground: I will pour my Spirit upon thy seed, and my blessing upon thine offspring: and they shall spring up as among the grass, as willows by the water courses."—ISA. xliv. 3, 4.

THESE words describe a time of refreshing.   There are no words in the whole Bible that have been oftener in my heart and oftener on my tongue than these, since I began my ministry among you.

And yet, although God has never, from the very first day, left us without some tokens of his presence, he has never fulfilled this promise; and I have taken it up to-day, in order that we may consider it more fully, and plead it more anxiously with God. For, as Rutherford said, " My record is on high, that your heaven would be like two heavens to me; and the salvation of you all, like two salvations to me."

I. *Who is the author of a work of grace?* It is God: "*I will pour.*"

1. It is God who *begins* a work of anxiety in dead souls. So it is in Zech. xii.: " I will pour out the Spirit of grace and supplications, and they shall look upon me whom they have pierced, and mourn." And so the promise is in John xvi.: " When he is come, he will convince the world of sin; because they believe not on me." And so is the passage of Ezek. xxxvii.: " Come from the four winds, O breath, and breathe upon these slain, that they may live." If any of you have been awakened, and made to beat upon the breast, it is God, and God alone, that hath done it. If ever we are to see a time of wide spread concern among your families—children asking their parents—parents asking their children—people asking their ministers, " What must I do to be saved ? "—if ever we are to see such a time as Edwards speaks of, when there was scarcely a single person in the whole town left unconcerned about the great things of the eternal world, God must pour out the Spirit: " I will pour."

2. It is God who *carries* on the work—leading awakened persons to Christ. " I will pour out my Spirit upon all flesh . . . and whosoever shall call upon the name of the Lord shall be delivered." (Joel ii. 28, 32.) And again, in John: " He shall convince the world of righteousness." If ever we are to see souls flying like a cloud, and like doves, to Jesus Christ—if ever we are to see multitudes of you fleeing to that city of refuge—if ever we are to see parents rejoicing over their children as new-born—husbands rejoicing over their wives, and wives over their husbands—God must pour out the Spirit. He is the author and finisher of a work of grace: " I will pour."

3. It is God who *enlarges* his people. You remember, in Zech. iv.,

13

how the olive trees supplied the golden candlesticks with oil—they emptied the golden oil out of themselves. If there is little oil, the lamps burn dim; if much oil, the lamps begin to blaze. Ah! if ever we are to see you who are children of God greatly enlarged, your hearts filled with joy, your lips filled with praises—if ever we are to see you growing like willows beside the water-courses, filled with all the fulness of God—God must pour down his Spirit—he must fulfil his word; for he is the Alpha and Omega, the author and finisher of a work of grace: " I will pour."

First Lesson.—Learn to look beyond ministers for a work of grace. God has given much honour to his ministers; but not the pouring out of the Spirit. He keeps that in his own hand: " I will pour." "It is not by might, nor by power, but by my Spirit, saith the Lord of hosts." Alas! we would have little hope, if it depended upon ministers; for where are our men of might now? God is as able to do it to-day as he was at the day of Pentecost; but men are taken up with ministers, and not with God. As long as you look to ministers, God cannot pour; for you would say it came from man. Ah! cease from man, whose breath is in his nostrils. One would think we would be humbled in the dust by this time. In how many parishes of Scotland has God raised up faithful men, who cease not day and night to warn every one with tears! and yet still the heavens are like brass, and the earth like iron. Why? Just because your eye is on man, and not on God. Oh! look off man to him, and he will pour; and his shall be all the glory.

Second Lesson.—Learn good hope of revival in our day.

Third Lesson.—Learn that we should pray for it. We are often for preaching to awaken others; but we should be more upon praying for it. Prayer is more powerful than preaching. It is prayer that gives preaching all its power. I observe that some Christians are very ready to censure ministers, and to complain of their preaching—of their coldness—their unfaithfulness. God forbid that I should ever defend unfaithful preaching, or coldness, or deadness, in the ambassador of Christ! May my right hand sooner forget its cunning! But I do say, where lies the blame of unfaithfulness?—where, but in the want of faithful praying? Why, the very hands of

14

Moses would have fallen down, had they not been held up by his faithful people. Come, then, ye wrestlers with God—ye that climb Jacob's ladder—ye that wrestle Jacob's wrestling—strive you with God, that he may fulfil his word: "I will pour."

II. *God begins with thirsty souls:* "I will pour water upon him that is thirsty."

1. *Awakened persons.*—There are often souls that have been a long time under the awakening hand of God. God has led them into trouble, but not into peace. He has taken them down into the wilderness, and there they wander about in search of refreshing waters; but they find none. They wander from mountain to hill seeking rest, and finding none—they go from well to well, seeking a drop of water to cool their tongue—they go from minister to minister, from sacrament to sacrament, opening their mouth, and panting earnestly; yet they find no peace. These are thirsty souls. Now, it is a sweet thought that God begins with such: "I will pour water upon him that is thirsty." The whole Bible shows that God has a peculiar tenderness for such as are thirsty. Christ, who is the express image of God, had a peculiar tenderness for them: "The Lord God hath given me the tongue of the learned, that I should know how to speak a word in season to him that is weary"—"Come unto me, all ye that are weary and heavy laden, and I will give you rest"—"If any man thirst, let him come unto me and drink." Many of his cures were intended to win the hearts of these burdened souls. The woman that had spent all upon other physicians, and was nothing better, but rather worse, no sooner touched the hem of his garment than she was made whole. Another cried after him: "Lord, help me," yet he answered not a word; but at last said: "O woman, great is thy faith; be it unto thee even as thou wilt." Another was bowed down eighteen years; but Jesus laid his hands on her, and immediately she was made straight.

Weary sinner! (1) This is Jesus; this is what he wants to do for you: "I will pour water upon him that is thirsty." Only believe that he is willing and able, and it shall be done. (2) Learn that it must come from his hand. In vain you go to other physicians; you

15

will be nothing better, but rather worse. Wait on him; kneel and worship him, saying: " Lord, help me." (3) Oh ! long for a time of refreshing, that weary souls may be brought into peace. If we go on in this every-day way, these burdened souls may perish—may sink uncomforted into the grave. Arise, and plead with God that he may arise and fulfil his word: " I will pour water upon him that is thirsty."

2. *Thirsty believers.* All believers should be thirsty; alas ! few are. Signs: (1) *Much thirst after the Word.* When two travellers are going through the wilderness, you may know which of them is thirsty, by his always looking out for wells. How gladly Israel came to Elim, where were twelve wells of water, and seventy palm trees ! So it is with thirsty believers; they love the Word, read and preached —they thirst for it more and more. Is it so with you, dear believing brethren ? In Scotland, long ago, it used to be so. Often, after the blessing was pronounced, the people would not go away till they heard more. Ah ! children of God, it is a fearful sign to see little thirst in you. I do not wonder much when the world stay away from our meetings for the Word and prayer; but, ah ! when you do, I am dumb—my soul will weep in secret places for your pride. I say, God grant that we may not have a famine of the Word ere long. (2) *Much prayer.* When a little child is thirsty for its mother's breast, it will not keep silence; no more will a child of God who is thirsty. Thirst will lead you to the secret well, where you may draw unseen the living water. It will lead you to united prayer. If the town were in want of water, and thirst was staring every man in the face, would you not meet one with another, and consult, and help to dig new wells ? Now, the town is in want of grace—souls are perishing for lack of it, and you yourselves are languishing. Oh ! meet to pray. " If two of you shall agree on earth as touching anything that they shall ask, it shall be done for them of my Father which is in heaven." (3) *Desire to grow in grace.* Some persons are contented when they come to Christ. They sink back, as it were, into an easy chair—they ask no more—they wish no more. This must not be. If you are thirsty believers, you will seek salvation as much after conversion as before it. " Forgetting those things which

16

are behind, and reaching forth unto those things which are before, I press toward the mark for the prize of the high calling of God in Christ Jesus."

To thirsty souls. Dear children, I look for the first drops of grace among you, in answer to your prayers, to fill your panting mouths. Oh, yes, he will pour. " A vineyard of red wine, I the Lord do keep it; I will water it every moment: lest any hurt it, I will keep it night and day." (Isa. xxvii. 2, 3.) " With joy shall ye draw water out of the wells of salvation." (Isa. xii. 3.)

III. *God pours floods on the dry ground.* The dry ground represents those who are dead in trespasses and sins. Just as you have seen the ground, in a dry summer, all parched and dry, cracking and open; yet it speaks not—it asks not the clouds to fall; so it is with most in our parishes. They are all dead and dry—parched and withered—without a prayer for grace—without even a desire for it. Yet what says God ? " I will pour floods upon them." Marks:—

1. *They do not pray.* I believe there are many in our parishes who do not make a habit of secret prayer—who, neither in their closet nor in the embowering shade, ever pour out their heart to God. I believe there are many who are dropping into hell who never so much as said: " God, be merciful to me a sinner." Ah ! these are the dry ground. Oh ! it is sad to think that the souls that are nearest to hell are the souls that pray least to be delivered from it.

2. *They do not wish a work of grace in their souls.* I believe many of you came to the house of God to-day who would rather lose house, and home, and friends, than have a work of grace done in your heart. Nothing would terrify you so much as the idea that God might make you a praying Christian. Ah ! you are the dry ground; you love death.

3. *Those who do not attend to the preached Word.* I have heard anxious persons declare that they never heard a sermon in all their life till they were awakened—that they regularly thought about something else all the time. I believe this is the way with many of you. You are the dry ground. What will God pour out on you ?

17

Floods—floods of wrath ? No; floods of grace—floods of the Spirit —floods of blessing. Oh! the mercy of God—it passes all understanding. You deserve the flood that came on the world of the ungodly; but he offers floods of blessing. You deserve the rain of Sodom; but, behold, he offers floods of his Spirit.

First Lesson.—Learn how much it is in your interests that there should be a work of grace in our day. You are the very persons who do not care about lively preaching—who ridicule prayer-meetings, and put a mock on secret prayer; and yet you are the very persons that are most concerned. Ah! poor dry-ground souls, you should be the first to cry out for lively ministers—you should go round the Christians, and, on your bended knees, entreat them to come out to our prayer-meeting. You, more than all the rest, should wait for the fulfilment of this word; for if it come not, oh! what will become of you ? Poor dead, dead souls, you cannot pray for yourselves! One by one, you will drop into a sad eternity.

Second Lesson.—Learn, Christians, to pray for floods. It is God's word—he puts it into your mouth. Oh! do not ask for drops, when God offers floods. " Open thy mouth and I will fill it."

IV. *Effects.*

1. Saved souls will be like grass. They shall spring up as grass. So, in Ps. lxxii.: "They of the city shall flourish like grass of the earth." Many will be awakened—many saved. At present, Christ's people are like a single lily amongst many thorns; but in a time of grace they shall be like grass. Count the blades of grass that spring in the clear shining after rain; so many shall Christ's people be. Count the drops of dew that come from the womb of the morning, shining like diamonds in the morning sun; so shall Christ's people be in a day of his power. Count the stars that sparkle in night's black mantle; so shall Abraham's seed be. Count the dust of the earth; so shall Israel be in the day of an outpoured Spirit. Oh! pray for an outpoured Spirit, ye men of prayer, that there may be many raised up in our day to call him blessed.

2. Believers shall grow like willows. There is nothing more distressing in our day than the want of growth among the

children of God. They do not seem to press forward—they do not seem to be running a race. When I compare this year with last year, alas ! where is the difference ?—the same weakness—the same coldness; nay, I fear, greater languor in divine things. How different when the Spirit is poured out ! They shall be like willows. You have seen the willow, how it grows—ceases not day or night—ever growing—ever shooting out new branches. Cut it down—it springs again. Ah ! so would you be, dear Christians, if there were a flood-time of the Spirit—a day of Pentecost. (1) Then there would be less care about your business and your workshop—more of prayer and of sweet praises. (2) There would be more change in you heart—victory over the world, the devil, and the flesh. You would come out, and be separate. (3) In affliction, you would grow in sweet submission—humility—meekness. There was a time in Scotland when Sabbath-days were growing days. Hungry souls came to' the Word, and went away filled with good things. They came like Martha, and went away like Mary. They came like Samson, when his locks were shorn, and went away like Samson when his locks were grown.

3. Self-dedication. " One shall say, I am the Lord's." Oh ! there is no greater joy than for a believing soul to give himself all to God. This has always been the way in times of refreshing. It was so at Pentecost. First they gave their ownselves unto the Lord. It was so with Boston, and Doddridge, and Edwards, and all the holy men of old. " I have this day been before God," says Edwards, " and have given myself—all that I am and have—to God; so that I am in no respect my own. I can challenge no right in myself—in this understanding, this will, these affections. Neither have I right to this body, or any of its members—no right to this tongue, these hands, these feet, these eyes, these ears. I have given myself clean away." Oh ! would that you knew the joy of giving yourself away. You cannot keep yourself. Oh ! this day try and give all to Him. Lie in his hand. Little children, O that you would become like him who said: " I am God's boy altogether, mother ! " Write on your hand: " I am the Lord's."

St. Peter's, July 1, 1838

19

THANKSGIVING OBTAINS THE SPIRIT[1]

" It came even to pass, as the trumpeters and singers were as one, to
make one sound to be heard in praising and thanking the Lord; and
when they lifted up their voice with the trumpets and cymbals and
instruments of music, and praised the Lord, saying, For he is good;
for his mercy endureth for ever: that then the house was filled with
a cloud, even the house of the Lord; so that the priests could not
stand to minister by reason of the cloud; for the glory of the Lord
had filled the house of God."—2 CHRON. v. 13, 14.

THE day here spoken of appears to have been a day of days. It
seems to have been the day of Pentecost in Old Testament times—a
type of all the glorious days of an outpoured Spirit that ever have
been in the world—a foretaste of that glorious day when God will
fulfil that amazing, soul-satisfying promise: " I will pour out my
Spirit upon all flesh."

My dearly beloved flock, it is my heart's desire and prayer that
this very day might be such a day among us—that God would
indeed open the windows of heaven, as he has done in times past, and
pour down a blessing, till there be no room to receive it.

Let us observe, then, how thanksgiving brings down the Spirit of
God.

I. *How the people were engaged:* " In praising and thanking the
Lord." Yea, you have their very words: " For he is good; for his
mercy endureth for ever." It was thus the people were engaged
when the cloud came down and filled the house. They had been
engaged in many other most affecting duties. The Levites had been
carrying the ark from Mount Zion and placing it under the wings of
the cherubim; Solomon and all his people had been offering sacrifices,
sheep and oxen, which could not be told for multitude—still no
answer came from heaven. But when the trumpeters and singers

---

[1] This sermon was preached at St. Peter's on the first Sabbath after his
return from Palestine, i.e. Nov. 24, 1839.

were as one in praising and thanking the Lord, when they lifted up their voices, saying: " For he is good; for his mercy endureth for ever "—then the windows of heaven were opened—then the cloud came down and filled the whole temple.

My dear flock, I am deeply persuaded that there will be no full, soul-filling, heart-ravishing, heart-satisfying, outpouring of the Spirit of God, till there be more praise and thanking the Lord. Let me stir up your hearts to praise.

1. *He is good.* Believers should praise God for what he is in himself. Those that have never seen the Lord cannot praise him. Those that have not come to Christ, have never seen the King in his beauty. An unconverted man sees no loveliness in God. He sees a beauty in the blue sky—in the glorious sun—in the green earth—in the spangling stars—in the lily of the field; but he sees no beauty in God. He hath not seen him, neither known him; therefore there is no melody of praise in that heart. When a sinner is brought to Christ, he is brought to the Father. Jesus gave himself for us, " that he might bring us to God." O ! what a sight breaks in upon the soul—the infinite, eternal, unchangeable God ! I know that some of you have been brought to see this sight. Oh ! praise him, then, for what he is. Praise him for his *pure, lovely holiness*, that cannot bear any sin in his sight. Cry, like the angels, " Holy, holy, holy, Lord God Almighty." Praise him for his *infinite wisdom*—that he knows the end from the beginning. In him are hid all the treasures of wisdom and knowledge. Praise him for his *power*—that all matter, all mind, is in his hand. The heart of the king, the heart of saint and sinner, are all in his hand. Hallelujah ! for the Lord God Omnipotent reigneth. Praise him for his *love*; for God is love. Some of you have been at sea. When far out of sight of land, you have stood high on the vessel's prow, and looked round and round— one vast circle of ocean without any bound. Oh ! so it is to stand in Christ justified, and to behold the love of God—a vast ocean all around you, without a bottom and without a shore. Oh ! praise him for what he is. Heaven will be all praise. If you cannot praise God, you never will be there.

2. *For his mercy—for what he has done for us.* The Lord has done

much for me since we parted. We were once in perils of waters; but the Lord saved the ship. Again and again we were in danger of plague—we nightly heard the cry of the mourner; yet no plague came near our dwelling. Again and again we were in perils of robbers—the gun of the murderous Arab has been levelled at us; but the Lord stayed his hand. I have been at the gates of death since we parted. No man that saw me would have believed that I could be here this day; yet he hath healed our diseases, and brought me back to open once more to you the unsearchable riches of Christ. I, then, have reason to praise him; for his mercy endureth for ever. The Lord has done much for you since we parted. My eyes filled with tears when I left you; for I thought he had done it in anger. I thought it was anger to me, and I thought it was anger to you; but now I see it was all love—it was all mercy to unworthy you and to unworthy me. The Lord gave you my dear brother to care for your souls; and far better than that—for to give you a man only would have been a poor gift—but he has given you his Holy Spirit. " Bless the Lord, O my soul ! " Praise him, O my people ! for he is good; for his mercy endureth for ever. Are there not some of you brands plucked out of the burning ? You were in the burning; the pains of hell were actually getting hold on you. You had a hell in your own hearts—you had a hell yawning to receive you; but the Lord snatched you from the burning. Will you not praise him ? Are there not some of you whom I left blind, and deaf, and dumb, and dead ? You saw no beauty in Him who is fairer than the children of men; you saw no glory in Immanuel—God manifest in flesh. But the Lord has said: " Go, wash in the pool of Siloam;" and whereas you were blind, now you see. Oh ! praise him that hath done it. In heaven, they praise God most of all for this: " Worthy is the Lamb that was slain." Oh ! have you no praise for Jesus for all his love—for the Father—for the Spirit ? Some of you cannot sing: " No man could learn that song but those that were redeemed from the earth." Some of you are worse than when I left you. You have resisted me—you have resisted my brother; and, oh ! worse than all, you have resisted the Holy Ghost. You are prayerless yet —Christless yet. Ah ! unhappy souls ! unredeemed, unrenewed,

22

remember it will be too late to learn to praise when you die. You must begin now. I will tell you what a dear friend of my own once said before dying. She desired all the servants to be brought in; and she said very solemnly: "There's nothing but Christ between me and weeping, and wailing, and gnashing of teeth. Oh! if you have not Christ, then there is nothing between you and weeping, and wailing, and gnashing of teeth." You that will not praise Christ now, shall wail because of him soon.

II. *The manner of their praise.*

They were "as one." Their hearts were all as one heart in this exercise. There were a thousand tongues, but only one heart. Not only were their harps, and cymbals, and dulcimers, all in tune, giving out a harmonious melody, but their hearts were all in tune. God had given them one heart, and then the blessing came down. The same was the case on the day of Pentecost; they were all with *one accord* in one place; they were looking to the same Lamb of God. The same thing will be the case in that day prophesied of in Psalm 133: "Behold, how good and how pleasant it is for brethren to dwell together in unity!—There God commands the blessing, even life for evermore." This is the very thing which Jesus prayed for in that prayer which none but God could have asked, and none but God could answer: "Neither pray I for these alone, but for them also which shall believe on me through their word; that they all may be one; as thou, Father, art in me, and I in thee, that they also may be one in us; that the world may believe that thou hast sent me." And then follows the blessing: "And the glory which thou gavest me I have given them; that they may be one, even as we are one: I in them, and thou in me, that they may be made perfect in one; and that the world may know that thou has sent me, and hast loved them, as thou hast loved me."

Dear children of God, unite your praises. Let your hearts no more be divided. You are divided from the world by a great gulf. Soon it will be an infinite gulf; but you are united to one another by the same Spirit—you have been chosen by the same free, sovereign love—you have been washed in the same precious blood—you have

23

been filled by the same blessed Spirit. Little children, love one another. He that loveth is born of God. Be one in your praises. Join in one cry: "Worthy is the Lamb that was slain: thou art worthy to open the book—thou art worthy to reign in our hearts." And, oh! be fervent in praise. Lift up your voices in it—lift up your hearts in it. In heaven they wax louder and louder. John heard the sound of a great multitude; and then it was like many waters, and then it was like mighty thunderings, crying: "Hallelujah! hallelujah!" I remember Edwards' remark, that it was in the singing of praises that his people felt themselves most enlarged, and that then God was worshipped somewhat in the beauty of holiness. Let it be so among yourselves. Learn, dearly beloved, to praise God heartily—to sing with all your heart and soul in the family and in the congregation. But, oh! remember that even your praises must be sprinkled with blood, and can be acceptable to God only by Jesus Christ.

III. *Effects.*

1. *The cloud filled the house.* This cloud is the very same which led them through the Red Sea, and went before them forty years in the wilderness. It was a pillar of cloud by day, to shade them from the heat; it was a pillar of fire by night, to guide Israel on their way to the promised rest; and now it came and filled the holiest of all and the holy place. Such was the wonderful effect which followed their united fervent praises. God himself came down, and filled every chamber of the house with his presence. "This is my rest for ever: here will I dwell; for I have desired it." Now, my dear friends, we are not now to expect that God will answer our prayers, or follow our praises, with a pillar of cloud or a pillar of fire. These were but the shadows; now we receive the reality—the substance. If ye will but unite in unanimous and heartfelt praises, then am I persuaded that God will give his Holy Spirit to fill this house—to fill every heart in the spiritual temple. How glorious this will be: (1) *For the children of God.* Are there not some of you who have come to Christ, and nothing more? Guilty, weary, heavy laden, you have found rest—redemption through his blood—even the for-

24

giveness of sins. Oh! do not stop there. Do not rest in mere forgiveness—cry for the indwelling of the Holy Ghost, the Comforter. Forgiveness is but a means to an end. You are justified in order that you may be sanctified. Remember, without holiness you will never see the Lord; and without this indwelling Spirit, you never will be holy.

Are there not some of you groaning under a body of sin and death, and crying, with the apostle, " Oh! wretched man, who shall deliver me from the body of this death ? " Do you not feel the plague of your own heart ? do you not feel the power of your old nature ? How many in this state lean upon themselves—trust in their resolutions—attempt, as it were, by force, to put down their sins ! But here is the remedy. Oh! cry for the flood-tide of God's Spirit, that he may fill every chamber of your heart—that he may renew you in the spirit of your mind.

Are there not many who are cold, worldly Christians—those who were long ago converted, but have fallen sadly back, under the power of the world—either its gaiety or its business, its mirth or its money—and they have got into worldly habits, deep ruts of sin ? Ah! see what you need. He that created man in his own image at first, must create you over again. You need an almighty indwelling Comforter. Oh! it is he only who can melt your icy heart, and make it flow out in love to God—who can fill you with all the fulness of God.

Are there not some who read the Bible, but get little from it ? You feel that it does not sink into your heart—it does not remain with you through the week. It is like the seed cast in the way-side, easily plucked away. Oh! it is just such an outpoured Spirit you require, to hide the Word in your heart. When you write with a dry pen, without any ink in it, no impression is made upon the paper. Now, ministers are the pens, and the Spirit of God is the ink. Pray that the pen may be filled with that living ink—that the Word may remain in your heart, known and read of all men—that you may be sanctified through the truth. (2) *For the unconverted*. So it was in the day of Pentecost—the Spirit came first upon the small company of disciples, and then on the three thousand. You have seen the hills attracting the clouds, and so drawing down the shower into the valleys—so do God's children, having their heads within the veil, obtain the Spirit of God in fulness, and dispense it to all around. You have seen some tall tree or spire catching the lightning, and conveying it down into the ground—so does the fire of God's Spirit come first upon the trees of righteousness, and from them descends to the dead souls around them.

A word to dead souls. Keep near to God's children at such a time as this. Do not separate from them—do not mock at them; you may yet receive the grace of God through them. Dear believers, for the sake of the dead souls around you—for the sake of this great town, full of wickedness—for the sake of our land, filled with formality and hypocrisy—oh! unite in prayer, and unite in praise, and prove the Lord, if he will not pour out a blessing. Not for your own sakes only, but for the sake of those perishing around you, let us wrestle and pray for a fuller time of the Spirit's working than has ever been seen in Scotland yet.

2. *The priests could not stand to minister.* Before the cloud came down, no doubt the priests were all busily engaged burning incense and offering sacrifices; but when the cloud came down, they could only wonder and adore. So it ever will be when the Lord gives much of his Spirit; he will make it evident that it is not the work of man. If he were to give only a little, then ministers would begin to think they had some hand in it; but when he fills the house, then he makes it plain that man has nothing to do with it. David Brainerd said, that when God awakened his whole congregation of Indians, he stood by amazed, and felt that he was as nothing—that God alone was working. Oh! it is this, dear friends, that we desire and pray for—that the Lord the Spirit would himself descend, and with his almighty power tear away the veil from your hearts, convince you of sin, of righteousness, and of judgment—that Jesus himself would take his sceptre and break your hard hearts, and take all the glory—that we may cry out: " Not unto us, Lord, not unto us, but unto thy name give glory."

FAMILY GOVERNMENT

" For I know him, that he will command his children and his household after him, and they shall keep the way of the Lord, to do justice and judgment; that the Lord may bring upon Abraham that which he hath spoken of him."—GEN. xviii. 19.

THERE are three things very remarkable in these words. 1. *That Abraham used parental authority in governing his family:* " I know him, that he will command his children and servants after him." He did not think it enough to pray for them, or to teach them, but he used the authority which God had given him—he commanded them. 2. *That he cared for his servants as well as his children.* In chapter xiv., verse 14, we learn that Abraham had three hundred and eighteen servants born in his house. He lived after the manner of patriarchal times; as the Arabs of the wilderness do to this day. His family was very large, and yet he did not say, " They are none of mine." He commanded his children and his household. 3. *His success:* " They shall keep the way of the Lord." It is often said that the children of good men turn out ill. Well, here is a good man, and a good man doing his duty by his children—and here is the result. His son Isaac was probably a child of God from his earliest years. There is every mark of it in his life. And what a delightful specimen of a believing, prayerful servant was Eliezer ! (Gen. xxiv.)

It is the duty of all believers to rule their houses well.

I. *The spring of this duty.*

1. *Love to souls.* As long as a man does not care for his own soul, he does not care for the souls of others. He can see his wife and children living in sin, going down to hell—he does not care. He does not care for missions—gives nothing to support missionaries. But the moment a man's eyes are opened to the value of his own

27

soul, that moment does he begin to care for the souls of others. From that moment does he love the missionary cause. He willingly spares a little to send the Gospel to the Jew and the perishing Hindus. Again, he begins to care for the Church at home—for his neighbours —all living in sin. Like the maniac at Decapolis, he publishes the name of Jesus wherever he goes. And now he begins to care for his own house. He commands his children and his household after him. How is it with you ? Do you rule well your own house ? Do you worship God, morning and evening, in your family ? Do you deal with your children and servants touching their conversion ? If not, you do not love their souls. And the reason is, you do not love your own. You may make what outward profession you please; you may sit down at sacrament, and talk about your feelings, but if you do not labour for the conversion of your children, it is all a lie. If you but felt the preciousness of Christ, you could not look upon their faces without a heart-breaking desire that they might be saved. Thus Rahab, Josh. ii. 13.

2. *Desire to use all talents for Christ.* When a man comes to Christ, he feels he is not his own. (1 Cor. vi. 19.) He hears Christ say: " Occupy till I come." If he be a rich man, he uses all for Christ, like Gaius. If a learned man, he spends all for Christ, like Paul. Now, parental authority is one talent—the authority of a master is another talent, for the use of which men will be judged. He uses these also for Christ. He commands his children and his household after him. How is it with you ? Do you use these talents for Christ ? If not, you have never given yourself away to him—you are not his.

II. *Scripture examples of it.*

1. *Abraham.* The most eminent example of it—the father of all believers. Are you a child of Abraham ? Then walk in his steps in this. Wherever Abraham went, he built an altar to the Lord.

2. *Job.* Upon every one of his son's birthdays Job offered sacrifice, according to the number of them all. (Chap. i. 5.)

3. *Joshua:* " As for me and my house, we will serve the Lord." (Chap. xxiv. 15.)

4. *Eunice.* From a child, little Timothy knew the Scriptures; and the reason for this you understand, when you read of the faith of his mother Eunice. (2 Tim. iii. 15, with i. 5.) Such was the manner in Scotland in the days of our fathers; and if ever we are to see Scotland again a garden of the Lord, it must be by the reviving of family government.

III. *The manner of it.*

1. *Worship God in your family.* If you do not worship God in your family, you are living in positive sin; you may be quite sure you do not care for the souls of your family. If you neglected to spread a meal for your children to eat, would it not be said that you did not care for their bodies ? And if you do not lead your children and servants to the green pastures of God's Word, and to seek the living water, how plain is it that you do not care for their souls ! *Do it regularly*, morning and evening. It is more needful than your daily food—more needful than your work. How vain and silly all your excuses will appear, when you look back from hell ! *Do it fully.* Some clip off the psalm, and some the reading of the Word; and so the worship of God is reduced to a mockery. *Do it in a spiritual, lively manner.* Go to it as to a well of salvation. There is, perhaps, no mean of grace more blessed. Let all your family be present without fail—let none be awanting.

2. *Command—use parental authority.* How awfully did God avenge it upon Eli, " because his sons made themselves vile, and he restrained them not " ! Eli was a good man, and a holy man; and often he spoke to his two wicked sons, but they heeded not. But herein he failed—he did not use his parental authority—he did not restrain them. Remember Eli. It is not enough to pray for your children, and to pray with them, and to warn them; but you must restrain them. Restrain them with the cords of love. From wicked books—from wicked companions—from wicked amusements—from untimely hours, restrain them.

3. *Command servants as well as children.* So did Abraham. Remember you are in the place of a father to your servants. They are come under your roof; and they have a claim on your instructions.

If they minister to you in carnal things, it is but fair that you minister to them in spiritual things. You have drawn them away from under the parental roof, and it is your part to see that they do not lose by it. Oh! what a mass of sin would be prevented, if masters would care for their servants' souls.

4. *Deal with each as to the conversion of his soul.* I have known many dear Christian parents who have been singularly neglectful in this particular. They worship God in the family, and pray earnestly in secret for their children and servants, and yet never deal with them as to their conversion. Satan spreads a kind of false modesty among parents, that they will not inquire of their little ones, Have you found the Lord, or no? Ah! how sinful and foolish this will appear in eternity. If you should see some of your children or servants in hell—all because you did not speak to them in private—how would you look? Begin to-night. Take them aside and ask, What has God done for your soul?

5. *Lead a holy life before them.* If all your religion is on your tongue, your children and servants will soon find out your hypocrisy.

IV. *The blessing which follows the performing of it.*

1. *You will avoid the curse.* You will avoid Eli's curse. Eli was a child of God, and yet he suffered much on account of his unfaithfulness. He lost his two sons in one day. If you would avoid Eli's curse, avoid Eli's sin. "Pour out thy fury on the families that have not called on thy name." (Jer. x. 25.) If you do not worship God in your house, a curse is written over your door. If I could mark the dwellings in this town where there is no family prayer—these are the spots where the curse of God is ready to fall. These houses are over hell.

2. *Your children will be saved.* So it was with Abraham. His dear son Isaac was saved. What became of Ishmael I do not know. Only I remember his fervent cry: "O that Ishmael might live before thee!" Such is the promise: "Train up a child in the way he should go, and when he is old he will not depart from it." Such is the promise in baptism. Ah! who can tell the blessedness of being the saved father of a saved family? Dear believers, be wise.

30

Surely if anything could mar the joy of heaven, it would be to see your children lost through your neglect. Dear unconverted souls, if one pang can be more bitter than another in hell, it will be to hear your children say: "Father, mother, you brought me here."

THE HEART DECEITFUL

"The heart is deceitful above all things, and desperately wicked: who can know it ? I the Lord search the heart, I try the reins, even to give every man according to his ways, and according to the fruit of his doings."—JER. xvii. 9, 10.

I. *The state of the natural heart.* (Verse 9.) This is a faithful description of the natural heart of man: The heart of unfallen Adam was very different. "God made man upright." His mind was clear and heavenly. It was riveted upon divine things. He saw their glory without any cloud or dimness. His heart was right with God. His affections flowed sweetly and fully towards God. He loved as God loved—hated as God hated. There was no deceit about his heart then. It was transparent as crystal. He had nothing to conceal. There was no wickedness in his heart—no spring of hatred, or lust, or pride. He knew his own heart. He could see clearly into its deepest recesses; for it was just a reflection of the heart of God. When Adam sinned, his heart was changed. When he lost the favour of God, he lost the image of God. Just as Nebuchadnezzar suddenly got a beast's heart, so Adam suddenly got a heart in the image of the devil. And this is the description ever since: "The heart is deceitful above all things, and desperately wicked." (Verse 9.)

1. *It is "deceitful above all things."* Deceit is one of the prime elements of the natural heart. It is more full of deceit than any other object. We sometimes call the sea deceitful. At evening

31

the sea appears perfectly calm, or there is a gentle ripple on the waters, and the wind blows favourably; during the night a storm may come on, and the treacherous waves are now like mountain billows, covering the ship. But the heart is deceitful *above all things*—more treacherous than the treacherous sea. The clouds are often very deceitful. Sometimes, in a time of drought, they promise rain; but they turn out to be clouds without rain, and the farmer is disappointed. Sometimes the clouds appear calm and settled; but, before the morning, torrents of rain are falling. But the heart is deceitful above all things. Many animals are deceitful. The serpent is more subtle than any beast of the field; sometimes it will appear quite harmless, but suddenly it will put out its deadly sting, and give a mortal wound. But the natural heart is more deceitful than a serpent—*above all things*. It is deceitful in two ways—in deceiving others and in deceiving itself.

(1) *In deceiving others.* Every natural man is a hypocrite. He is different in reality from what he appears to be. I undertake to say, that there is not a natural man present here to-day in his true colours. If every natural man here were to throw off his disguise, and appear as he really is, this church would look more like the gate of hell than the gate of heaven. If every unclean man were to lay bare his heart, and show his abominable, filthy desires and thoughts; if every dishonest man were now to open his heart, and let us see all his frauds, all his covetous, base desires; if every proud, self-conceited one were now to show us what is going on below his coat, or below that silk gown—to let us see the paltry schemes of vanity and desire of praise; if every unbeliever among you were openly to reveal his hatred of Christ and of the blessed Gospel—O what a hell would this place appear! Why is it not so? Because natural men are deceitful—because you draw a cloak over your heart, and put on a smooth face, and make the outside of a saint cover the heart of a fiend. Oh! your heart is deceitful above all things. Every natural man is a flatterer. He does not tell other men what he thinks of them. There is no plain, honest dealing between natural men in this world. Those of you who know anything of this world, know how hollow most of its friendships are. Just imagine for a moment

that every natural man were to speak the truth when he meets his friends; suppose he were to tell them all the bitter slanders which he tells of them a hundred times behind their back; suppose he were to unbosom himself, and tell all his low, mean ideas of them—how worldly and selfish they are in his eyes;—alas! what a world of quarrels this would be. Ah, no! natural man, you dare not be honest—you dare not speak the truth one to another; your heart is so vile that you must draw a cloak over it; and your thoughts of others so abominable that you dare not speak them out: "The heart is deceitful above all things."

(2) It shows itself in another way—in self-deceit. Ever since my coming among you I have laboured with all my might to separate between the precious and the vile. I have given you many marks, by which you might know whether or not you have undergone a true conversion, or whether it has only been a deceit of Satan—whether your peace was the peace of God or the peace of the devil—whether you were on the narrow way that leads to life, or on the broad way that leads to destruction. I have done my best to give you the plainest Scripture marks by which you might know your real case; and yet I would not be in the least surprised, if the most of you were found at the last to have deceived yourselves. Often a man is deeply concerned about his soul; he weeps and prays, and joins himself to others who are inquiring. He now changes his way of life, and changes his notions; he talks of his experience, and enlargement in prayer; perhaps he condemns others very bitterly; and yet he has no true change of life—he walks after the flesh still, not after the Spirit. Now, others think this man a true Christian, and he believes it himself; yea, he thinks he is a very eminent Christian; when, all the time, he has not the Spirit of Christ, and is none of his. Ah! "the heart is deceitful above all things."

2. "*Desperately wicked.*" This word is borrowed from the book of the physician. When the physician is called to see a patient, past recovery, he shakes his head and says: This is a desperate case. This is the very word used here. "The heart is desperately wicked"—past cure by human medicine. *Learn that you need conversion, or a new heart.* When we speak of the necessity of a

change to some people, they begin to be affected by it, and so they put away some evil habits, as drinking or swearing, or lying; they put these away, and promise never to go back to them; and now they think the work is done, and they are in a fair way for heaven. Alas, foolish man! it is not your drinking, or your swearing, or your lying that are desperately wicked—but your heart. You have only been cutting off the streams—the source remains polluted—the heart is as wicked as ever. It is the heart that is incurable. It is a new heart you need. Nothing less will answer your need. *Learn that you must go to Christ for this.* When the woman had spent her all upon physicians, and was nothing better, but rather worse, she heard of Jesus. Ah! said she, if I may but "touch the hem of his garment I shall be made whole." Jesus said to her: "Daughter, be of good comfort, thy faith hath made thee whole." Come, then, incurable, to Christ. The leprosy was always regarded as incurable. Accordingly, the leper came to Jesus, and worshipping, said: "Lord, if thou wilt thou canst make me clean." Jesus said, "I will, be thou clean"; and immediately his leprosy was cleansed. Some of you feel that your heart is desperately wicked; well, kneel to the Lord Jesus, and say: "Lord, if thou wilt, thou canst make me clean." You are a leper—incurable; Jesus is able—he is also willing to make you clean.

3. *Unsearchably wicked: "Who can know it?"* No man ever yet knew the badness of his own heart. We are sailing over a sea the depths of which we have never fathomed. (1) *Unawakened persons* have no idea of what is in their hearts. When Elisha told Hazael what a horrible murderer he would be, Hazael said: "Is thy servant a dog, that he should do this great thing?" The seeds of it were all in his heart at that moment; but he did not know his own heart. If I had told some of you, when you were little children playing beside your mother's knee, the sins that you were afterwards to commit, you would have said: "Am I a dog, that I should do this thing?" and yet you see you have done them. If I could show each of you the sins that you are yet to commit, you would be shocked and horrified. This shows how ignorant you are of your own heart. I suppose that the most of you think it quite impossible you should

ever be guilty of murder, or adultery, or apostasy, or the sin against the Holy Ghost; this arises from ignorance of your own black heart: "*Who can know it?*" (2) *Some awakened persons* have an awful sight given them of the wickedness of their own hearts. They see all the sins of their past life, as it were, concentrated there. They see that their past sins all come out of their heart—and that the same may come out again. And yet the most awakened sinner does not see the ten thousandth part of the wickedness of his heart. You are like a person looking down into a dark pit—you can only see a few yards down the sides of the pit; so you can only see a little way down into your heart. It is a pit of corruption which is bottomless: "*Who can know it?*" (3) *Some children of God* have amazing discoveries given them of the wickedness of their own hearts. Sometimes it is given them to see that the germs of every sin are lodging there. Sometimes they see that there never was a sin committed, in heaven, in earth, or in hell, but it has something corresponding to it in their own heart. Sometimes they see that if there were not another fountain of sin, from which the fair face of creation might be defaced, their own heart is a fountain inexhaustible—enough to corrupt every creature, and to defile every fair spot in the universe. And yet even they do not know their own hearts. You are like a traveller looking down into the crater of a volcano; but the smoke will not suffer you to look far. You see only a few yards into the smoking volcano of your own heart.

Learn to be humbled far more than you have ever been. None of you have ever been sufficiently humbled under a sense of sin; for this reason, that none of you have ever seen fully the plague of your own heart. There are chambers in your heart you have never yet seen into—there are caves in that ocean you have never fathomed—there are fountains of bitterness you have never tasted. When you have felt the wickedness of your heart to the uttermost, then lie down under this awful truth, that you have only seen a few yards into a pit that is bottomless—that you carry about with you a slumbering volcano—a heart whose wickedness you do not and cannot know.

II. *The witness of the heart.*

1. "*I, the Lord.*" We have seen that we do not know one another's hearts; for "the heart is deceitful." Man looketh on the outward appearance. We have seen that no man knows his own heart—that the most know nothing of what is there; and those who know most, see but a short way down. But here is an unerring witness. He that made man knows what is in man.

2. *Observe what a strict witness he is:* "I, the Lord, search the heart, I try the reins." It is not said, I *know* the heart—but, I *search* it. The heart of man is not one of the many objects upon which God turns his all-seeing eye, but it is one which he singles out for investigation: "I search the heart." As the astronomer directs his telescope upon the very star he wishes to examine, and arranges all his lenses, that he may most perfectly look at it; so doth God's calm eye pore upon the naked breast of every man. As the refiner of silver keeps his eye upon the refining pot, watching every change in the boiling metal; so doth God's eye watch every change in the bosom of man. Oh! natural man, can you bear this? How vain are all your pretences and coverings! God sees you as you are. You may deceive your neighbour, or your minister, or yourself—but you cannot deceive God.

3. *Observe, he is a constant witness.* He does not say, I have searched, or I will do it—but, I *search*—I do it now, and always. Not a moment of our life but his pure, calm, searching eye has been gazing on the inmost recesses of our hearts. From childhood to old age his eye rests on us. The darkness hideth not from him. The darkness and the light are both alike to him.

4. *Observe his end in searching:* "Even to give every man according to his ways, and according to the fruit of his doings." (Verse 10.) In order to know the true value of an action, you must search the heart. Many a deed that is applauded by men, is abominable in the sight of God, who searches the heart. To give an alms to a poor man, may be an action either worthy of an eternal reward, or worthy of an eternal punishment. If it be done out of love to Christ—because the poor man is a disciple of Christ—it will in no wise lose its reward; Christ will say: "Inasmuch as ye did it to the

36

least of these my brethren, ye did it unto me." If it be done out of pride or self-righteousness, Christ will cast it from him; he will say, "Depart, ye cursed—ye did it not unto me." The reason, then, why Christ searches the heart is, that he may judge uprightly in the judgment. Oh, sirs! how can you bear this, you that are Christless? How can you bear that eye on your heart all your days, and to be judged according to what his pure eye sees in you? Oh! do you not see it is a gone case with you? "Enter not into judgment with thy servant; for in thy sight shall no flesh living be justified." Oh! if your heart be desperately wicked, and his pure eye ever poring on it, what can you expect, but that he should cast you into hell? Oh! flee to the Lord Jesus Christ for shelter—for blood to blot out past sins, and righteousness to cover you.

Learn the amazing love of Christ. He was the only one that knew the wickedness of the beings for whom he died. He that searches the hearts of sinners died for them. His eye alone had searched their hearts; ay, was searching at the time he came. He knew what was in men; yet he did not abhor them on that account—he died for them. It was not for any goodness in man that he died for man. He saw none. It was not that he saw little sin in the heart of man. He is the only being in the universe that saw all the sin that is in the unfathomable heart of man. He saw to the bottom of the volcano—and yet he came and died for man. Herein is love! When publicans and sinners came to him on earth, he knew what was in their hearts. His eye had rested on their bosoms all their life—he had seen all the lusts and passions that had ever rankled there; yet in no wise did he cast them out. So with you. His eye hath seen all your sins—the vilest, darkest, blackest hours you have lived, his pure eye was resting on you; yet he died for such, and invites you to come to him; and will in no wise cast you out.

CHRIST'S LOVE TO THE CHURCH

" Husbands, love your wives, even as Christ also loved the Church, and
gave himself for it; that he might sanctify and cleanse it with the
washing of water by the Word, that he might present it to himself a
glorious Church, not having spot, or wrinkle, or any such thing; but
that it should be holy and without blemish."—EPH. v. 25–27.

IN this passage the apostle, under the guidance of the Spirit, is
teaching wives and husbands their duties to one another. To the
wives he enjoins submission—a loving yielding to their husbands in
all lawful things; to the husbands, love; and he puts before them the
highest of all patterns—Christ and his Church.

I. *Christ's love to his Church.*
1. *The object of his love.* The Church—all who are chosen,
awakened, believing, justified, sanctified, glorified—all who are
finally saved—all who shall stand with the Lamb—the hundred and
forty and four thousand redeemed ones—all looked on as the bright
company; the Church—all who are awakened and brought to
Christ—all who shall sit down at the marriage supper. I believe
Jesus had compassion for the whole world. He is not willing that
any should perish. He willeth all men to be saved. He shed tears
over those who will finally perish. Still, the peculiar object of his
love was the Church. He loved the Church. On them his eye
rested with peculiar tenderness before the world was. He would
often say: These shall yet sit with me on my throne; or, as he read
over their names in his book of life, he would say: These shall yet
walk with me in white. When they lived in sin, his eye was upon
them. He would not let them die, and drop into hell: " I have
much people in this city." I have no doubt, brethren, Christ is
marking some of you that are now Christless, for his own. When
they came to Christ, he let out his love toward them on the land

38

where they dwelt—a delightsome land. His eye rests on the houses of this town, where his jewels live. Christ loves some streets far better than others—some spots of earth are far dearer to him than others.

Christ loved his Church. Just as a husband at sea loves the spot where his dear wife dwells, so does the Lord Jesus: " I have graven thee upon the palms of my hands." (Isa. xlix. 16.) He loves some in one house far more than others. There are some apartments dear to Christ—where he is often present—where his hands are often on the door: " Open to me, my love."

2. *The state of the Church when first loved.* (1) They were all under the curse of God—under condemnation—exposed to the just wrath of God—deserving nothing but wrath; for " he gave himself for it." The Church had no dowry to attract the love of Jesus, except her wrath and curse. (2) *Impure.* For he had to " sanctify and cleanse it"; unholy within—opposed to God—no beauty in the eye of Jesus: I am black, spotted, and wrinkled. (3) *Nothing to draw the love of Christ.* Nothing that he could admire in them. He admires whatever is like his Father. He had eternally gazed upon his Father, and was ravished with that beauty; but he saw none of this—not a feature—no beauty at all. Men love where they see something to draw esteem—Christ saw none. (4) *Everything to repel his love:* " Polluted in thine own blood "—cast out—loathsome (Ezek. xvi.); yet that was the time of his love. Black—uncomely: " Thou hast loved me out of the pit of corruption." (5) *Not from ignorance.* Men often love where they do not know the true character, and repent after. But not so Christ. He knew the weight of their sins—the depths of their wicked heart.

Nothing is more wonderful than the love of Christ. *Learn the freeness of the love of Christ.* It is unbought love. " If a man would give all the substance of his house for love, it would utterly be contemned." (Song viii. 7.) He drew all his reasons from himself: " I knew that thou wast obstinate." You have no cause to boast. He loved you, because he loved you—for nothing in you. O what a black soul wast thou, when Christ set his love upon thee !

3. *The greatness of that love:* " He gave himself." This is un-

paralleled love. Love is known by the sacrifice it will make. In a fit of love, Herod would have given away the half of his kingdom. If you 'will sacrifice nothing, you love not. Hereby we know that men love not Christ—they will sacrifice nothing for him. They will not leave a lust—a game—a companion, for Christ. " Greater love than this hath no man." But Christ gave himself. Consider what a self. If he had created ten thousand millions of worlds, and given them away, it had been great love—had he given a million of angels; but he gave the Lord of angels—the Creator of worlds. " Lo, I come." He gave the pearl of heaven. O what a self !—Jesus !— all loveliness !

4. *What he gave himself to.* He gave himself to be put in their place—to bear their wrath and curse, and to obey for them. We shall never know the greatness of this gift. He gave himself to bear the guilt of the Church. There cannot be a more fearful burden than guilt, even if there be no wrath. To the holy soul of Jesus, this was an awful burden. He was made sin: " Mine iniquities have taken hold upon me, so that I am not able to look up." (Ps. xl.) " Mine iniquities are gone over mine head : as a heavy burden, they are too heavy for me." (Ps. xxxviii.) He endured the cross, despising the shame. He laid his soul under their guilt—shame and spitting; silent like a lamb.

To bear their wrath. A happy soul shrinks from suffering. Ask one that has always been in the love of God, what would he give to cast himself out of that love—bear as much wrath as he is bearing love—to receive the lightning instead of the sunshine ? Not for ten millions of worlds. Yet this did Jesus. He became a curse for us : See how he shrank back from it in the garden. Yet he drank it.

"God commendeth his love to us, in that, while we were yet sinners, Christ died for us." Pray to know the love of Christ. It is a great ocean, without bottom or shore.[1] In the broken bread you will see it set forth so that a child may understand : " This is my body, broken for you "—" This is my blood, shed for many."

[1] " It is as if a child could take the globe of earth and sea in his two short arms."—SAMUEL RUTHERFORD.

40

II. *His purpose in time.* (Verse 26.) Christ's work is not done with a soul when he has brought it to pardon—when he has washed it in his own blood. Oh, no ! the better half of salvation remains—his great work of sanctification remains.

1. *Who is the author ?* He that gave himself for the Church— the Lamb that was slain. God having raised his Son Jesus, sent him to bless you, in turning every one of you away from your iniquities. He is exalted by the right hand of God, and, having obtained the promise of the Father, sheds him down. There is no hand can new-create the soul, but the hand that was pierced. Many look to a wrong quarter for sanctification. They take pardon from Christ, then lean on themselves—their promises—for holiness. Ah, no ! you must take hold of the hand that was pierced—lean on the arm that was racked—lean on the Beloved coming up from the wilderness. You might as well hold up the sun on its journey, as sanctify yourself. It needs divine power. There are three con- cerned in it. The Father—for this is his will; the Son- -he is the Shepherd of all he saves; the Holy Ghost.

2. *The means:* " The Word." I believe he could sanctify without the Word, as he created angels and Adam holy, and as he sanctifies infants whose ear was never opened; but I believe in grown men he never will, but through the Word. When Jesus makes holy, it is by writing the Word in the heart: " Sanctify them through thy truth." When a mother nurses her child, she not only bears it in her arms, but holds it to her breast, and feeds it with the milk of her own breast; so does the Lord. He not only holds the soul, but feeds it with the milk of the Word. The words of the Bible are just the breathings of God's heart. He fills the heart with these, to make us like God. When you go much with a companion, and hear his words, you are gradually changed by them into his likeness; so when you go with Christ, and hear his words, you are sanctified. Oh, there are some whom I could tell to be Christ's, by their breathing the same sweet breath ! Those of you that do not read your Bible cannot turn like God—you cannot be saved. You are unsavable; you may turn like the devil, but you never will turn like God. Oh, believers, prize the Word !

41

3. *The certainty of it.* Some are afraid they will never be holy: " I shall fall under my sin." You shall be made holy. *It was for this Christ died.* This was the grand object he had in view. This was what was in his eye—to build a holy Church out of a world of lost sinners—to pluck brands out of the fire, and make them trees of righteousness—to choose poor, black souls, and make them fair brothers and sisters round his throne. Christ will not lose this object.

Look up, then—be not afraid. He redeemed you to make you holy. Though you had a million of worlds opposing you, he will do it: " He is faithful, who also will do it."

III. *His purpose in eternity—twofold.*

1. *Its perfection:* " A glorious Church." At present believers are sadly imperfect. They have on the perfect righteousness that will be no brighter above; but they are not perfectly holy; they mourn over a body of sin—spots and wrinkles. Neither are they perfectly happy. They are often crushed; waves of trouble go over them. But they shall be perfectly glorious. Perfect in righteousness— White robes, washed in the blood of the Lamb. Perfect in holiness— Filled with the Holy Spirit. Perfect in happiness—This shall be. It is all in the covenant.

2. *He will present it to himself.*—He will be both Father and Bridegroom. He has bought the redeemed—he will give them away to himself. The believer will have great nearness—he shall see the King in his beauty. Great intimacy—walk with him—speak with him. He shall have oneness with him—" All that I have is thine."

St. Peter's, Jan. 3, 1841.

MY GOD, MY GOD

" My God, my God, why hast thou forsaken me ? "—MATT. xxvii. 46.

THESE are the words of the great Surety of sinners, as he hung upon the accursed tree. The more I meditate upon them, the more impossible do I find it to unfold all that is contained in them. You must often have observed how a very small thing may be an index of something great going on within. *The pennant* at the mast-head is a small thing; yet it shows plainly which way the wind blows. *A cloud* no bigger than a man's hand is a small thing; yet it may show the approach of a mighty storm. *The swallow* is a little bird; and yet it shows that summer is come. *So is it with man.* A look— a sigh—a half-uttered word—a broken sentence—may show more of what is passing within than a long speech. *So it was with the dying Saviour.* These few troubled words tell more than volumes of divinity.

May the Lord enable us to find something here that will feed your souls.

I. *The completeness of Christ's obedience.*

1. *Words of obedience:* " My God, My God." He was obedient unto death. I have often explained to you how the Lord Jesus came to be a doing as well as a dying Saviour—not only to suffer all that we should have suffered, but to obey all that we should have obeyed —not only to suffer the curse of the law, but to obey the commands of the law. When the thing was proposed to him in heaven, he said: " Lo, I come to do thy will, O my God ! "—" Yea, thy law is within my heart." Now, then, look at him as a man obeying his God. See how perfectly he did it—even to the last ! God says: Be about my business—he obeys: " Wist ye not that I must be about my Father's business ? " God says: Speak to sinners for

me—he obeys: " I have meat to eat that ye know not of; my meat is to do the will of him that sent me, and to finish his work." God says: Die in the room of sinners—wade through a sea of my wrath for the sake of enemies—hang on a cross, and bleed and die for them —he obeys: " No man taketh my life from me." The night before he said: " The cup which my Father hath given me, shall I not drink it ? " But perhaps he will shrink back when he comes to the cross ? No; for three hours the darkness has been over him, yet still he says: " My God, my God." Sinner, do you take Christ as your surety ? See how fully he obeyed for thee ! The great command laid upon him was to die for sinners. Behold how fully he obeys !

2. *Words of faith:* " My God, my God." These words show the greatest faith that ever was in this world. Faith is believing the word of God, not because we see it to be true, or feel it to be true, but because God has said it. Now Christ was forsaken. He did not see that God was his God—he did not feel that God was his God; and yet he believed God's word, and cried: " My God, my God." (1) *David* shows great faith in Ps. xlii. 7, 8: " Deep calleth unto deep at the noise of thy waterspouts: all thy waves and thy billows are gone over me. Yet the Lord will command his loving-kindness in the daytime, and in the night his song shall be with me, and my prayer unto the God of my life." He felt like one covered with a sea of troubles. He could see no light—no way of escape; yet he believed the word of God, and said: " Yet the Lord will." This is faith—believing when we do not see. (2) Jonah showed great faith: " All thy billows and thy waves passed over me; then I said, I am cast out of thy sight; yet I will look again toward thy holy temple." (Jonah ii. 3, 4.) He was literally at the bottom of the sea. He knew no way of escape—he saw no light—he felt no safety; yet he believed the word of God. This was great faith. (3) *But, ah ! a greater than Jonah is here.* Here is greater faith than David's —greater faith than Jonah's—greater faith than ever was in the world, before or after. Christ was now beneath a deeper sea than that which covered Jonah. The tossing billows of God's anger raged over him. He was forsaken by his Father—he was in outer

44

darkness—he was in hell; and yet he believed the word of God. " Thou wilt not leave my soul in hell." He does not feel it—he does not see it—but he believes it, and cries: " My God." Nay, more, to show his confidence, he says it twice: " My God, my God." " Though he slay me, yet will I trust in him." Dear believer, this is your surety. You are often unbelieving—distrustful of God; behold your surety—he never distrusted; cling to him—you are complete in him.

3. *Words of love.* " My God, my God." Those were words of sweet submission and love which Job spake, when God took away from him property and children: " Naked came I out of my mother's womb," &c. Sweet, that he could bless God even in taking away from him. Those were words of sweet submissive love which old Eli spake, when God told him that his sons should die: " It is the Lord, let him do what seemeth him good." The same sweet temper was in the bosom of the Shunammite who lost her child, when the prophet asked: " Is it well with thee ?—is it well with thy husband ? —is it well with the child ? And she answered, It is well." But, ah ! here is greater love—greater, sweeter submission, than that of Job, or Eli, or the Shunammite—greater than ever was breathed in this cold world before. Here is a being hanging between earth and heaven—forsaken by his God—without a smile—without a drop of comfort—the agonies of hell going over him; and yet he loves the God that has forsaken him. He does not cry out, Cruel, cruel Father !—no, but with all the vehemence of affection, cries out, " My God, my God." Dear, dear souls, is this your surety ? Do you take him as obeying for you ? Ah ! then, you are complete in him. You have very little love for God. How often you have murmured, and thought God cruel in taking things away from you; but, behold your surety, and rejoice in him with exceeding joy. All the merit of his holy obedience is imputed to you.

II. *The infinity of Christ's sufferings.* He was forsaken by God: " My God, my God, why hast thou forsaken me ? " The Greek Liturgy says: " We beseech thee, by all the sufferings of Christ, known and unknown." The more we know of Christ's sufferings,

45

the more we see that they cannot be known. Ah ! who can tell the full meaning of the broken bread and poured-out wine ?

1. *He suffered much from his enemies.* (1) He suffered in all parts of his body. In his head—that was crowned with thorns, and smitten with the reed. In his cheeks—for they smote him on the face, and he gave his cheeks to them that plucked off the hair: " I hid not my face from shame and spitting." In his shoulders—that carried the heavy cross. In his back: " I gave my back to the smiters." In his hands and feet: " They pierced my hands and my feet." In his side—a soldier thrust a spear into his side. Ah ! how well he might say: " This is my body, broken for you." (2) He suffered in all his offices. As a prophet: " They smote him on the face and said, Prophesy who smote thee." As a priest—they mocked him when offering up that one offering for sins. As a king, when they bowed the knee, and jesting said, " Hail ! king of the Jews." (3) He suffered from all sorts of men—from priests and elders—from passers by and soldiers—from kings and thieves: " Many bulls have compassed me; strong bulls of Bashan have beset me round "—" Dogs have compassed me "—" They compassed me about like bees." (4) He suffered much from the devil: " Save me from the lion's mouth." His whole suffering was one continued wrestling with Satan; for he " spoiled principalities and powers, and made a show of them openly, triumphing over them in his cross."

2. *He suffered much from those he afterwards saved.* How bitter would be the scoffing of the thief who that day was to be forgiven and accepted ! How bitter the cries of the three thousand who were so soon brought to know him whom they crucified !

3. *From his own disciples.* They all forsook him and fled. John, the beloved, stood afar off, and Peter denied him. It is said of the camomile flower, that the more you squeeze and tread upon it, the sweeter is the odour it spreads around. Ah ! so it was in our sweet Rose of Sharon. It was the bruising of the Saviour that spread sweet fragrance around. It is the bruising that makes his name as ointment poured forth.

4. *From his Father.* All other sufferings were nothing in com-

parison with this: " My God, my God, why hast thou forsaken me ?"
Other sufferings were finite—this alone was an infinite suffering.
It was little to be bruised by the heel of men or devils; but, ah ! to
be trodden by the heel of God: " It pleased the Father to bruise
him."

Three things show the infinity of his sufferings.

1. *Who it was that forsook him.* Not his people Israel—not
Judas the betrayer—not Peter his denier—not John that lay in his
bosom—he could have borne all this; but, ah ! it was his Father
and his God. Other things little affected him compared with that.
The passers by wagged their heads—he spoke not. The chief
priests mocked him—he murmured not. The thieves cast it in his
teeth—he was as a deaf man who heareth not. God brought a three
hours' darkness over him—the outward darkness being an image
of the darkness over his soul—ah ! this was infinite agony: " My
God, my God, why hast *thou* forsaken me ? "

2. *Who it was that was forsaken:* " *Me.*" (1) One infinitely dear
to God. Thou lovedst me before the foundation of the world, yet
thou hast forsaken me. I was always by thee—rejoicing always
before thee. I have basked in the beams of thy love. Ah ! why
this terrible darkness to *me* ? " My God, my God." (2) One who
had an infinite hatred of sin. How dreadful to an innocent man
to be thrust into the cell of a condemned criminal ! but, ah ! how
much more dreadful to Christ, who had an infinite hatred of sin, to
be regarded by God as a sinner. (3) One who had an infinite relish
of God's favour. When two friends of exalted minds meet together,
they have an intense relish of one another's love. How painful to
meet the cold averted looks of one in whose favour you find this
sweet joy ! But, ah ! this is nothing to Christ's pain.

3. *What God did to him—forsook him.* Dear friends, let us look
into this ocean through which Christ waded. (1) He was without
any comforts of God—no feeling that God loved him—no feeling
that God pitied him—no feeling that God supported him. God
was his sun before—now that sun became all darkness. Not a
smile from his Father—not a kind look—not a kind word. (2) He
was without a God—he was as if he had no God. All that God had

47

been to him before was taken from him now. He was Godless—deprived of his God. (3) He had the feeling of the condemned, when the Judge says: "Depart from me, ye cursed," "who shall be punished with everlasting destruction from the presence of the Lord, and from the glory of his power." He felt that God said the same to him. Ah! this is the hell which Christ suffered. Dear friends, I feel like a little child casting a stone into some deep ravine in the mountain side, and listening to hear its fall—but listening all in vain; or like the sailor casting the lead at sea, but it is too deep—the longest line cannot fathom it. The ocean of Christ's sufferings is unfathomable.

III. Answer the Saviour's *why*.

Because he was the surety of sinners, and stood in their room.

1. *He had agreed with his Father*, before all worlds, to stand and suffer in the place of sinners: Every curse that should fall on them, let it fall on me. Why should he be surprised that God poured out all his fury? "Why hast thou forsaken me?" Because thou didst covenant to stand in the room of sinners.

2. *He set his face to it:* "He set his face like a flint"—"He set his face stedfastly." God set down the cup before him in the garden, saying, "Art thou willing to drink it, or no?" He said: "The cup which my Father hath given me, shall I not drink it?" "Therefore it pleased the Lord to bruise him." Why? Because thou hast chosen to be the surety—thou wouldst not draw back.

3. *He knew that either he or the whole world must suffer.* It was his pity for the world made him undertake to be a Saviour: "He saw that there was no man, and wondered that there was no intercessor. Therefore his arm brought salvation unto him, and his righteousness it sustained him." Why? Either thou or they—hell for thee or hell for them.

1. *Lesson to Christless persons.* Learn your danger. Wherever God sees sin he will punish it. He punished it in the rebellious angels—in Adam—in the old world—in Sodom; and when he saw sins laid on Christ, he forsook his own Son. You think nothing of sin. See what God thinks of it. If so much as one sin be upon you

uncovered, you cannot be saved. God says: "Though thou wert the signet on my right hand—though thou wert the son of my bosom—yet would I pluck thee hence." Oh, let me persuade you, this day, to an immediate closing with Jesus Christ !

2. *Lesson to the people of Christ.* Admire the love of Jesus. Oh, what a sea of wrath did he lie under for you ! Oh, what hidings did he bear for you, vile, ungrateful soul ! The broken bread and poured-out wine are a picture of his love. Oh, when you look on them, may your heart break for longing toward such a Saviour !

We would say to all who close with Jesus Christ, He was forsaken in the room of sinners. If you close with him as your surety, you will never be forsaken. From the broken bread and poured-out wine seems to rise the cry: " My God, my God, why hast thou forsaken me ? "

For *me*—for *me*. May God bless his own Word.

TIME IS SHORT

" But this I say, brethren, the time is short: it remaineth, that both they that have wives be as though they had none; and they that weep, as though they wept not; and they that rejoice, as though they rejoiced not; and they that buy, as though they possessed not; and they that use this world, as not abusing it: for the fashion of this world passeth away."—1 Cor. vii. 29–31.

IN this chapter the apostle is discoursing concerning marriage. The mind of God upon this subject seems to be—1. *That in ordinary times marriage is honourable in all, provided it be in the Lord.* There are some who seem to imagine that there is peculiar holiness about an unmarried life; but this seems quite contrary to the Word of God. In the sinless world before man fell, God said: " It is not good for man to be alone;" and the closest walker with God in Old Testament times was a married man: " Enoch walked with God three hundred years, and begat sons and daughters." 2. *That in a time of distress and trouble to the Church it is better not to marry:* " I suppose therefore that this is good for the present distress." (Verse 26.) When the ark of God is in danger, as at present in our Church, it seems the mind of the Spirit, that all who can should keep themselves as much as possible disentangled from earthly engagements. When the wife of Phinehas heard that the ark of God was taken, she travailed in birth, and died, calling her child Ichabod—The glory is departed. So, brethren, it does not become those who love Zion to be marrying and giving in marriage when the ark of God is in danger. 3. *That even in such times it is lawful to marry:* " But and if thou marry, thou hast not sinned." (Verse 28.) I doubt not, brethren, the days are near when they shall say: " Blessed are the barren, and the wombs that never bare, and the paps that never gave suck." Still, if any will venture to meet these times, and if you think the faith of two may bear you up better than the faith of one, " *I spare you.*" I would lay no snare upon you. You have not sinned.

Having opened up this subject, the apostle proceeds with this affecting statement, suitable to all, married or unmarried: " But this I say, brethren, the time is short: it remaineth that both they that have wives be as though they had none; and they that weep, as though they wept not; and they that rejoice, as though they rejoiced not; and they that buy, as though they possessed not; and they that use this world, as not abusing it: for the fashion of this world passeth away." In these words there is—1. *A statement made:* " The time is short;" and again: " The fashion of this world passeth away." The time to be spent in this world is very short; it is but an inch of time—a short half-hour. In a very little, it will be all over; and all that is here is changing—the very hills are crumbling down—the loveliest face is withering away—the finest garments rot and decay: " The fashion of this world passeth away." 2. *A lesson drawn from this:* Believers should sit loose to everything here. Believers should look on everything in the light of eternity. Value nothing any more than you will do then. Sit loose to the objects, griefs, joys, occupations of this world; for you must soon change them for eternal realities.

50

Doctrine.—The shortness of time should make believers sit loose to all things under the sun.

I. *The shortness of time.* True in two respects.

1. *The time a believer has to live in this world is very short.* (1) *The whole lifetime is very short.* From the cradle to the grave is but a short journey: " The days of our years are threescore years and ten; and if by reason of strength they be fourscore years, yet is their strength labour and sorrow; for it is soon cut off, and we fly away." The half of men die before the age of twenty. Even when men lived for many hundred years, it was but a short life—a moment, compared to eternity. Methuselah lived nine hundred and sixty-nine years, and he died. Men are shortlived, like the grass. " All flesh is as grass;" and the rich and beautiful are like the flower of the field— a little fairer and more delicate. " The grass withereth, the flower fadeth; because the Spirit of the Lord bloweth upon it." (Isa. xl. 7.) " For what is your life ? It is even a vapour, that appeareth for a little time, and then vanisheth away." (James iv. 14.) You know how swiftly a weaver's shuttle flies; but your life flies more swiftly: " My days are swifter than a weaver's shuttle." (Job vii. 6.) " My days are swifter than a post; they are passed away as the swift ships; as the eagle that hasteth to the prey." (Job ix. 25, 26.) (2) *How much is already passed away.* Most believers spent their first days in sin. Many hearing me gave their best days to sin and the world. Many among you have only the lame, and the torn, and the sick, to give to God. All of you can look on the past as a sleep, or as a tale that is told. The time since I came among you appears to me just like a dream. (3) *What remains is all numbered.* All of you hearing me have your Sabbaths numbered—the number of sermons you are to hear. The last one is already fixed upon. Your years are numbered. To many this is the last year they shall ever see in this world. Many will celebrate their next new year in glory. The disease is now in the body of many of you that is to lay you in the dust; and your grave is already marked out. In a little while you will be lying quietly there. Yes, dear brethren, " *the time is short.*"

2. *The time of this world's continuance is short:* " The end of all

things is at hand "—" The fashion of this world passeth away."
A believer stands on a watch-tower—things present are below his
feet—things eternal are before his eyes. A little while, brethren,
and the day of grace will be over—preaching, praying will be done.
Soon we shall give over wrestling with an unbelieving world—soon
the number of believers shall be complete, and the sky open over
our heads, and Christ shall come. His parting cry was: "Surely
I come quickly." Then we shall see him "whom, having not seen,
we loved." A little while, and we shall stand before the great white
throne; a little while, and the wicked shall not be—we shall see them
going away into everlasting punishment; a little while, and the work
of eternity shall be begun. We shall be like him—we shall see him
day and night in his temple—we shall sing the new song, without
sin and without weariness, for ever and ever. In a little moment,
brethren, all this shall be: "For a small moment have I hid my face
from thee; but with everlasting mercies will I gather thee."

II. *The believer should learn from this to sit loose to all things under
the sun.*

1. *Sit loose to the dearest objects of this world:* "It remaineth,
therefore, that they who have wives be as though they had none."
Marriage is honourable in all. Husbands should love their wives,
even as Christ loved the Church: "So ought men to love their wives
as their own bodies." Still it must not be idolatry. A married
believer should be, in some respects, as if he were unmarried—as if
he had no wife. "Honour thy father and thy mother, that thy
days may be long upon the land which the Lord thy God giveth
thee." You cannot be too kind, too gentle, too loving, to the
parents whom God has given you; yet be as though you had none.
Parents, love your children, and bring them up in the nurture and
admonition of the Lord; yet feel that the time is short. They are
only a loan from the Lord. Be not surprised if he take his own.
Esteem your ministers highly in love, for their work's sake; yet be
as if you had none. Lean as entirely on Christ as if you had never
seen or heard a minister. Brainerd mentions an instance of one
woman, who, after her conversion, was resigned to the divine will

in the most tender points: " What if God should take away your husband from you—how do you think you would bear that ? " She replied: " He belongs to God, and not to me; he may do with him just what he pleases." When she longed to die, to be free from sin, she was asked what would become of her infant; she answered, " God will take care of it; it belongs to him—he will take care of it." Rutherford says: " Build your nest upon no tree here; for you see God hath sold the forest to Death, and every tree whereon we would rest is ready to be cut down, to the end we may flee and mount up, and build upon the Rock, and dwell in the holes of the Rock." Set not your heart on the flowers of this world; for they have all a canker in them. Prize the Rose of Sharon and the Lily of the Valley more than all; for he changeth not. Live nearer to Christ than to the saints, so that when they are taken from you, you may have him to lean on still.

2. *Sit loose to the griefs of this world.* They that weep should be as though they wept not. This world is the vale of tears. There are always some mourning. No sooner is the tear dried up on one cheek that it trickles down another. No sooner does one widow lay aside her weeds, than another takes them up. Those that are in Christ should weep as though they wept not; " for the time is short." Do you weep over those that died in the Lord ? It is right to weep: " Jesus wept." Yet weep as though you wept not; " for the time is short." They are not lost, but gone before. The sun, when it sets, is not lost; it is gone to shine in another hemisphere; and so have they gone to shine in a brighter world. It is self-love that makes you mourn for them; for they are happy. You would not mourn if they were with a distant friend on earth—why do you mourn that they are with the sinner's Friend ? " They shall hunger no more, neither thirst any more, neither shall the sun light upon them, nor any heat; for the Lamb which is in the midst of the throne shall feed them, and shall lead them unto fountains of living waters; and God shall wipe away all tears from their eyes." (Rev. vii. 16, 17.) " The time is short;" and you will follow after. A few days, and you may be leaning together on the bosom of Jesus; you are nearer them to-day than you were yesterday. " The time is short;"

and you will meet with all the redeemed at the right hand of Christ—we shall mingle our voices in the new song, and wave together the eternal palm ! " Weep as though you wept not."

Do you weep over those that died out of the Lord ? Ah ! there is deeper cause for weeping here; and yet the time is short, when all this will be explained to you, and you will not be able to shed a tear over the lost. A little while, and you will see Jesus fully glorified, and you will not be able to wish anything different from what has happened. When Aaron lost his two sons, he held his peace.

Do you mourn over bodily pain, and poverty, and sickness, and the troubles of the world ? Do not murmur: " The time is short." If you have believed in Christ, these are all the hell you will ever bear. Think you the dying thief would complain of his pains when he was within a step of paradise ? So it is with you. Your hell is dried up, and you have only these two shallow brooks to pass through —sickness and death; and you have a promise that Christ shall do more than meet you—go with you, foot for foot, and bear you in his arms. When we get to the presence of Jesus, all our griefs shall look like children's griefs: a day in his presence will make you remember your miseries no more. Wherefore take courage, and run with patience.

3. *Sit loose to the enjoyments of this world.*

It is quite right for a believer to use the things of this world, and to rejoice in them. None has such a right as the believer has to rejoice and be happy. He has a right to use the bodily comforts of this world—to eat his meat " with gladness and singleness of heart, praising God." He has a right to all the joys of home, and kindred, and friendship. It is highly proper that he should enjoy these things. He has a right to all the pure pleasures of mind, of intellect, and imagination; for God has given him all things richly to enjoy. Still, he should " rejoice as though he rejoiced not, and use this world as not abusing it;" for " the time is short." In a little while, you will be at your Father's table above, drinking the new wine with Christ. You will meet with all your brothers and sisters in Christ—you will have pure joy in God through ceaseless ages. Do not be much taken with the joys that are here. I have noticed children, when they were going out to a feast, they would eat but sparingly, that they might have a keener appetite for the coming dainties; so, dear friends, you are going to a feast above, do not dull your appetite with earthly joys—sit loosely to them all—look upon them all as fading. As you walk through a flower garden, you never think of lying down, to make your home among its roses; so, pass through the garden of this world's best joys. Smell the flowers in passing; but do not tarry. Jesus calls you to his banqueting house—there you will feed among the lilies on the mountains of spices. Oh! it ill becomes a child of God to be fond of an earthly banquet, when you are looking to sitting down so soon with Jesus—it ill becomes you to be much taken up with dress and show, when you are so soon to see the face that was crowned with thorns. Brethren, if you are ever so much taken up with any enjoyment that it takes away your love for prayer or for your Bible, or that it would frighten you to hear the cry: " The Bridegroom cometh;" and you would say: Is he come already ? then you are abusing this world. Oh! sit loose to this world's joy: " The time is short."

4. *Sit loose to the occupations of the world.* It is right for Christians to be diligent in business. I often wonder how unconverted souls can be so busy—how, when you are bustling along, filling up all your time with worldly things, it never occurs to you that there will be none of this in eternity. How can I be so busy for my body, when my poor soul is unprovided for ? But those in Christ may well be diligent. (1) They have a good conscience—that oils the wheels. " A merry heart doeth good like a medicine." A light heart makes easy work. (2) They love to honour their Lord. They would not have it said that a believer in Jesus was an idler or a sluggard—the love of Jesus constrains them to all that is lovely. And yet a believer should " buy as though he possessed not;" for " the time is short." Oh! believers, ye cannot be misers; for you are but stewards. All that you possess here is your Lord's; and the day is at hand when he will transfer you to take care of another property in a brighter land. You are but servants. It would not do if you were to set your hearts on the things of this lower room; for in a few days the Master is to call you to serve in his own dear presence.

Dear believers, be ready to leave your room for the golden harp, at a minute's warning; be ready to leave your desk for the throne of Jesus—your pen for the palm of victory; be ready to leave the market below, for the street of the new Jerusalem, where the redeemed shall walk. If you were in a sinking ship, you would not cling hard to bags of money—you would sit loose to all, and be ready to swim. This world is like a sinking ship, and those who grasp at its possessions will sink with it. Oh ! " buy as though you possessed not;" for " the time is short."

III. *What the unconverted should learn from the shortness of time.*
1. *Learn your folly in having lost the past.* Although life be very short, it is all saving time. This is the reason for which God has given it to us. The long-suffering of God is intended for our salvation. God gives men time to hear the Gospel—to pray—to get saving conversion. But unconverted souls have wasted all the past. Think how much time you have lost in idleness. How many golden opportunities for prayer, and hearing the Word, and meditation, have you lost ! how much time have you spent uselessly in your bed, or in idle talk, or in loitering about your doors ! If you saw how short your time is, and how death and hell are pursuing you, you would have fled to Christ; but you have not. Think how much you have spent in sin, at the tavern, or in vain company, or in dances, or in night walking, or in sins of which it is a shame even to speak. God gave you time for saving your soul, and you have spent it in ruining your soul. God gave you time to flee to Christ; and you have spent it in fleeing toward hell. Think how much time you have spent in business, without one thought for eternity. Think how you have lost your best time. Youth is your best time of being saved. Many of you have lost it. Time of awakening—Sabbaths—holy time—years of Sabbaths have now gone over many of you. " The harvest is past, the summer is ended; and we are not saved."
2. *Consider what value they put on time who are now in hell.* Once, brethren, they cared as little for it as you—once, they could see their years pass away without caring—once, they could let their

Sabbaths slip away; but now they see their folly. What would they now give, brethren, for such an opportunity as you have this day ? What would they give for another year of grace—for another week—for another day ? It is probable that some of your friends or companions, now in hell, are wishing they could come back to tell you how precious is an inch of saving time !

Oh ! brethren, be wise. " Why stand ye all the day idle ? " It has come to the eleventh hour with some—your unconverted head is grey—your feet are tottering. If you saw a man condemned to die, lying in chains, who had but three hours to live; if you saw that man playing at dice, or singing wanton songs, would you not be shocked ? You would say he was a hardened wretch. Ah ! are there none among you the same ? You are condemned already—your days are numbered—you are hanging by a thread over the mouth of hell; and yet you are cutting and slashing at the hand that holds you. In a little moment, brethren, it will be all over. Throughout the never-ending ages of eternity you will remember the few days we spent together. Ah ! the remembrance will add fuel to the flame, and be a never-dying worm in your poor soul.

I SLEEP, BUT MY HEART WAKETH

" I sleep, but my heart waketh: it is the voice of my beloved that knocketh, saying, Open to me, my sister, my love, my dove, my undefiled: for my head is filled with dew, and my locks with the drops of the night," &c.—SONG OF SOLOMON v. 2–16.

THE passage I have read forms one of the dramatical songs of which this wonderful book is composed. The subject of it is a conversation between a forsaken and desolate wife and the daughters of Jerusalem. First of all, she relates to them how, through slothfulness, she had turned away her lord from the door. He had been absent on a journey from home, and did not return till night.

Instead of anxiously sitting up for her husband, she had barred the door, and slothfully retired to rest: "I slept, but my heart was waking." In this half-sleeping, half-waking frame, she heard the voice of her beloved husband: "Open to me, my sister, my love, my dove, my undefiled; for my head is filled with dew, and my locks with the drops of the night." But sloth prevailed with her, and she would not open, but answered him with foolish excuses: "I have put off my coat; how shall I put it on? I have washed my feet; how shall I defile them?"

2. She next tells them her grief and anxiety to find her lord. He tried the bolt of the door, but it was fastened. This wakened her thoroughly. She ran to the door and opened, but her beloved had withdrawn himself, and was gone. She listened—she sought about the door—she called—but he gave no answer. She followed him through the streets; but the watchmen found her, and smote her, and took away her veil; and now with the morning light she appears to the daughters of Jerusalem, and anxiously beseeches them to help her: "I charge you, if ye find him whom my soul loveth, that ye tell him that I am sick of love."

3. The daughters of Jerusalem, astonished at her extreme anxiety, ask: "What is thy beloved more than another beloved?" This gives opportunity to the desolate bride to enlarge on the perfections of her lord, which she does in a strain of the richest descriptiveness— the heart filling fuller and fuller as she proceeds, till she says: "This is my beloved, and this is my friend, O ye daughters of Jerusalem!" they seem to be entranced by the description, and are now as anxious as herself to join in the search after this altogether lovely one. "Whither is thy beloved gone, O thou fairest among women? whither is thy beloved turned aside, that we may seek him with thee?"

Such is the simple narrative before us. But you will see at once that there is a deeper meaning beneath—that the narrative is only a beautiful transparent veil, through which every intelligent child of God may trace some of the most common experiences in the life of the believer. (1) The desolate bride is the believing soul. (2) The daughters of Jerusalem are fellow-believers. (3) The watchmen are ministers. (4) And the altogether lovely one is our Lord and Saviour Jesus Christ.

I. *Believers often miss opportunities of communion with Christ through slothfulness.*

1. *Observe, Christ is seeking believers.* It is true that Christ is seeking unconverted souls. He stretches out his hands all the day to a gainsaying and disobedient people—he is the Shepherd that seeks the lost sheep; but it is as true that he is seeking his own people also —that he may make his abode with them—that their joy may be full. Christ is not done with a soul when he has brought it to the forgiveness of sins. It is only then that he begins his regular visits to the soul. In the daily reading of the Word, Christ pays daily visits to sanctify the believing soul. In daily prayer, Christ reveals himself to his own in another way than he doth to the world. In the house of God Christ comes to his own, and says: " Peace be unto you ! " And in the sacrament he makes himself known to them in the breaking of bread, and they cry out: " It is the Lord ! " These are all trysting times, when the Saviour comes to visit his own.

2. *Observe, Christ also knocks at the door of believers.* Even believers have got doors upon their hearts. You would think, perhaps, that when once Christ had found an entrance into a poor sinner's heart, he never would find difficulty in getting in any more. You would think that as Samson carried off the gates of Gaza, bar and all, so Christ would carry away all the gates and bars from believing hearts; but no, there is still a door on the heart, and Christ stands and knocks. He would fain be in. It is not his pleasure that we should sit lonely and desolate. He would fain come into us, and sup with us, and we with him.

3. *Observe, Christ speaks:* " Open to me, my sister, my love, my dove, my undefiled." O what a meeting of tender words is here !— all applied to a poor sinner who has believed in Christ. (1) " My sister; " for you remember how Jesus stretched his hand toward his disciples, and said: " Behold my mother and my brethren; for whosoever shall do the will of my Father, the same is my brother, and my sister, and my mother." (2) " My love; " for you know

59

how he loved sinners—left heaven out of love—lived, died, rose again, out of love, for poor sinners; and when one believes on him he calls him " My love." (3) " My dove;" for you know that when a sinner believes in Jesus, the holy dove-like Spirit is given him; so Jesus calls that soul " My dove." (4) " My undefiled "—strangest name of all to give to a poor defiled sinner. But you remember how Jesus was holy, harmless, and undefiled. He was that in our stead—when a poor sinner believes in him, he is looked on as undefiled. Christ says: " My undefiled." Such are the winning words with which Christ desires to gain an entrance into the believer's heart. Oh, how strange that any heart could stand out against all this love !

4. *Observe, Christ waits:* " My head is filled with dew, and my locks with the drops of the night." Christ's patience with unconverted souls is very wonderful. Day after day he pleads with them: " Turn ye, turn ye, why will ye die ? " Never did beggar stand longer at a rich man's gate, than Jesus, the almighty Saviour, stands at the gate of sinful worms. But his patience with his own is still more wonderful. They know his preciousness, and yet will not let him in. Their sin is all the greater, and yet he waits to be gracious.

5. *Believers are often slothful at these trysting times, and put the Saviour away with vain excuses.* (1) The hour of daily devotion is a trysting hour with Christ, in which he seeks, and knocks, and speaks, and waits; and yet, dear believers, how often are you slothful, and make vain excuses ! You have something else to attend to, or you are set upon some worldly comfort, and you do not let the Saviour in. (2) The Lord's table is the most famous trysting-place with Christ. It is then that believers hear him knocking—saying: " Open to me." How often is this opportunity lost through slothfulness—through want of stirring up the gift that is in us—through want of attention—through thoughts about worldly things—through unwillingness to take trouble about it !

    " I have put off my coat; how shall I put it on ?
    I have washed my feet; how shall I defile them ? "

Doubtless, there are some children of God here, who did not find Christ last Sabbath-day at his table—who went away unrefreshed and uncomforted. See here the cause—it was your own slothfulness. Christ was knocking; but you would not let him in. Do not go about to blame God for it. Search your own heart, and you will find the true cause. Perhaps you came without deliberation—without self-examination and prayer—without duly stirring up faith. Perhaps you were thinking about your worldly gains and losses, and you missed the Saviour. Remember, then, the fault is yours, not Christ's. He was knocking—you would not let him in.

II. *Believers in darkness cannot rest without Christ.*

In the parable we find that, when the bride found her husband was gone, she did not return to her rest. Oh, no ! her soul failed for his word. She listens—she seeks—she calls. She receives no answer. She asks the watchmen, but they wound her, and take away her veil; still she is not broken off from seeking. She sets the daughters of Jerusalem to seek along with her.

So is it with the believer. When the slothful believer is really awakened to feel that Christ has withdrawn himself, and is gone, he is slothful no longer. Believers remain at ease only so long as they flatter themselves that all is well; but if they are made sensible, by a fall into sin, or by a fresh discovery of the wickedness of their heart, that Christ is away from them, they cannot rest. The world can rest quite well, even while they know that they are not in Christ. Satan lulls them into fatal repose. Not so the believer—he cannot rest. 1. He does all he can do himself. He listens—he seeks—he calls. The Bible is searched with fresh anxiety. The soul seeks and calls by prayer; yet often all in vain. He gets no answer—no sense of Christ's presence. 2. He comes to ministers—God's watchmen on the walls of Zion. They deal plainly and faithfully with the backslidden soul—take away the veil and show him his sin. The soul is thus smitten and wounded, and without a covering; and yet it does not give over its search for Christ. A mere natural heart would fall away under this—not so the believer in darkness. 3. He applies to Christian friends and companions—bids them help him, and pray for him: " I charge you, O ye daughters of Jerusalem, if ye find him whom my soul loveth, tell him that I am sick of love."

61

Is there any of you, then, a believer in darkness, thus anxiously seeking Christ? You thought that you had really been a believer in Jesus; but you have fallen into sin and darkness, and all your evidences are overclouded. You are now anxiously seeking Christ. Your soul fails for his Word. You seek, you call, even though you get no answer. You do search the Bible, even though it is without comfort to you. You do pray, though you have no comfort in prayer—no confidence that you are heard. You ask counsel of his ministers; and when they deal plainly with you, you are not offended. They wound you, and take away the veil from you. They tell you not to rely on any past experiences—that they may have been delusive—they only increase your anxiety; still you follow hard after Christ. You seek the daughters of Jerusalem—them that are the people of Christ—and you tell them to pray for you.

Is this your case? As face answers to face, so do you see your own image here? Do you feel that you cannot rest out of Christ? then do not be too much cast down. This is no mark that you are not a believer, but the very reverse. Say:—

> " Why art thou cast down, O my soul?
> Why art thou disquieted in me?
> Still trust in God; for I shall yet praise him,
> Who is the health of my countenance, and my God."

Is there any of you awakened, since last Sabbath-day, by some fall into sin, to feel that Christ is away from you? Doubtless, there must be some who, within this little week, have found out that, though they ate bread with Christ, they have lifted up the heel against him. And are you sitting down contented—without anxiety? Have you fallen, and do you not get up and run, that, if possible, you may find Christ again? Ah, then! I stand in doubt of you; or rather, there is no need of doubt—you have never known the Saviour—you are none of his.

III. *Believers in darkness are sick of love, and full of the commendation of Christ—more than ever.*

In the parable, the bride told the daughters of Jerusalem that she was sick of love. This was the message she bade them carry; and when they asked her about her beloved, she gave them a rich and glowing description of his perfect beauty, ending by saying: " He is altogether lovely."

So it is with the believer in time of darkness: " He is sick of love." When Christ is present to the soul, there is no feeling of sickness. Christ is the health of the countenance. When I have him full in my faith as a complete surety, a calm tranquillity is spread over the whole inner man—the pulse of the soul has a calm and easy flow—the heart rests in a present Saviour with a healthy, placid affection. The soul is contented with him—at rest in him: " Return unto thy rest, O my soul." There is no feeling of sickness. It is health to the bones; it is the very health of the soul to look upon him, and to love him. But when the object of affection is away, the heart turns sick. When the heart searches here and there, and cannot find the beloved object, it turns faint with longing: " Hope deferred maketh the heart sick." When the ring-dove has lost its mate, it sits lone and cheerless, and will not be comforted. When the bird that hath been robbed of its young, comes back again and again, and hovers with reluctant wing over the spot where her nest was built, she fills the grove with her plaintive melodies—she is " sick of love." These are the yearnings of nature. Such also are the yearnings of grace. When Jesus is away from the believing soul it will not be comforted. When the soul reads, and prays, and seeks, yet Jesus is not found, the heart yearns and sickens—he is " sick of love." " Hope deferred maketh the heart sick."

Did you ever feel this sickness ? Did you ever feel that Christ was precious, but not present—that you could not lay hold on Christ as you used to do, and yet your soul yearned after him, and would not be comforted without him ? If you have—1. Remember it is a happy sickness—it is a sickness not of nature at all, but of grace. All the struggles of nature would never make you " sick of love." Never may you be cured of it, except it be in the revealing of Jesus ! 2. Remember it is not best to be " sick of love "—it is better to be in health—to have Christ revealed to the soul, and to love him with a free, healthy love. In heaven, the inhabitants never say they are

63

sick. Do not rest in this sickness; press near to Jesus to be healed.

3. Most, I fear, never felt this sickness—know nothing of what it means. Oh! dear souls, remember this one thing: If you never felt the sickness of grace, it is too likely you never felt the life of grace. If you were told of a man, that he never felt any pain or uneasiness of any kind all his days, you would conclude that he must have been dead—that he never had any life; so you, if you know nothing of the sick yearnings of the believer's heart, it is too plain that you are dead—that you never had any life.

Last of all, the believer in darkness commends the Saviour. There is no more distinguishing mark of a true believer than this. To the unawakened there is no form nor comeliness in Christ—no beauty that they should desire him. Even awakened souls have no true sense of Christ's perfect comeliness. If they saw how Christ answers their need, they could not be anxious. But to believers in darkness there is all comeliness in Christ—he is fairer than ever he was before. And when the sneering world, or cold-hearted brethren, ask: " What is thy beloved more than another beloved ? " he delights to enumerate his perfections, his person, his offices, his everything: he delights to tell that " he is the chiefest among ten thousand "— " his mouth is most sweet "—yea, " he is altogether lovely."

A word to believers in darkness. There may be some who are walking in darkness, not having any light. Be persuaded to do as the bride did—not only to seek your beloved, but to commend him, by going over his perfections.

1. Because this is the best of all ways to find him. One of the chief reasons of your darkness is your want of considering Christ. Satan urges you to think of a hundred things before he will let you think about Christ. If the eye of your faith be fully turned upon a full Christ, your darkness will be gone in the instant. " Look unto me, and be ye saved." Now, nothing so much engages your eye to look at Christ as going over his perfections to others.

2. Because you will lead others to seek him with you. Oh! dear brethren, the great reason of our having so many dark Christians now-a-days is, that we have so many selfish Christians. Men live for themselves. If you would live for others, then your darkness

would soon flee away. Commend Christ to others, and they will go with you. Parents, commend him to your children; children, commend him to your parents, and who knows but God may bless the word, even of a believer walking in darkness, that they shall cry out:

" Whither is thy beloved gone, O thou fairest among women ?
Whither is thy beloved turned aside, that we may seek him with thee ? "

THE SECOND COMING OF CHRIST

" For the Son of Man is as a man taking a far journey, who left his house, and gave authority to his servants, and to every man his work, and commanded the porter to watch. Watch ye therefore: for ye know not when the master of the house cometh, at even, or at midnight, or at cockcrowing, or in the morning: lest coming suddenly he find you sleeping. And what I say unto you, I say unto all, Watch."—MARK xiii. 34–37.

I. *The Church on earth is Christ's house:* " Who left his house." This parable represents the Church on earth as Christ's house or dwelling.

1. *Because he is the foundation stone of it.* Just as every stone of a building rests on the foundation, so does every believer rest on Christ. He is the foundation rock upon which they rest. If it were not for the foundation, the whole house would fall into ruins— the floods and winds would sweep it away. If it were not for Christ, all believers would be swept away by God's anger; but they are rooted and built up in him, and so they form his house.

2. *Because he is the builder.* (1) Every stone of the building has been placed there by the hands of Christ—Christ has taken every stone from the quarry. Look unto the rock whence ye were hewn, and the hole of the pit whence ye were digged. A natural person is embedded in the world just as firmly as a rock in the quarry. The hands of the almighty Saviour alone can dig out the soul, and loosen it from its natural state. (2) Christ has carried it, and laid it on the foundation. Even when a stone has been quarried, it cannot lift itself; it needs to be carried, and built upon the foundation. So when a natural soul has been wakened, he cannot build himself on Christ; he must be carried on the shoulder of the great master builder. Every stone of the building has been thus carried by Christ. What a wonderful building ! Well may it be called Christ's house, when he builds every stone of it. See that ye be quarried out by Christ; see to it, that ye be carried by him—built on him; then you will be an habitation of God through the Spirit.

3. *Because his friends are in it.* Wherever a man's friends are, that is his home—wherever a man's mother and sister and brother dwell, that is his home; this, then, must be Christ's home, for he stretched forth his hand toward his disciples, and said: " Behold my mother and my brethren; for whosoever shall do the will of my Father which is in heaven, the same is my brother, and sister, and mother." As long as this world has a believer in it, Christ will look upon it as his house. He cannot forget, even in glory, the well of Samaria—the garden of Gethsemane—the hill of Calvary. Happy for you who know Christ, and who do the will of his Father; wherever you dwell, Christ calls it his house. You may dwell in a poor place, and still be happy; for Christ dwells with you, and calls it his dwelling—he calls you " My brother, sister, mother."

II. *Christ is like a man who has gone a far journey.* (Verse 34.) Although the Church on earth be his house, and although he has such affection for it, yet Christ is not here, he is risen—Christ is risen indeed.

1. *He has gone to take possession of heaven in our name.* When an elder brother of a family purchases a property for himself and his brothers, he goes a far journey, in order to take possession. So

Christ is an elder brother. He lived and died in order to purchase forgiveness and acceptance for sinners. He has gone into heaven to take possession for us. Do you take Christ for your surety ? Then you are already possessed of heaven.

Ques. How am I possessed of heaven, when I have never been there ?

Ans. Christ your surety has taken possession in your name. If you will realize this, it will give you fulness of joy. A person may possess a property which he has never seen.

Look at your surety in the land that is very far off, calling it all his own, for the sake of his younger brethren: " These things have I spoken unto you, that your joy may be full."

2. *He has gone to intercede for us.* (1) He has gone to intercede for unawakened, barren sinners: " Lord, let it alone this year also." Oh, sinner ! why is it that you have not died a sudden death ? Why have you not gone quite down into the pit ? How often the Saviour has prayed for some of you ! Shall it be all in vain ? (2) To intercede for his believing people—to procure all blessings for them. Often an elder brother of a family goes into a far country, and sends back rich presents to his younger brethren at home. This is what Christ has done. He has gone far above all heavens, there to appear in the presence of God for us, and to ask the very things we need, and to send us down all the treasures of heaven. Of his fulness have we all received, even grace for grace. " I will pray the Father, and he shall give you another Comforter." Oh, Christians ! believe in a praying Christ, if you would receive heavenly blessings. Believe just as if you saw him, and open the mouth wide to receive the blessings for which he is praying.

3. *He has gone to prepare a place for us.* When a family are going to emigrate to a foreign shore, often the elder brother goes before to prepare a place for his younger brethren. This is what Christ has done. He does not intend that we should live here always—he has gone a far journey in order to prepare a place for us: " I go to prepare a place for you; and if I go and prepare a place for you, I will come again and receive you to myself, that where I am, there ye may be also." Oh, Christians ! believe in Christ preparing a place

for you. It will greatly take away the fear of dying. It is an awful thing to die, even for a forgiven and sanctified soul—to enter on a world unknown, unseen, untried. One thing takes away fear: Christ is preparing a place quite suitable for my soul—he knows all the wants and weaknesses of my frame—I know he will make it a pleasant home to me.

III. *All Christ's people are servants, and have their work assigned them.* (Verse 34.)

1. *Ministers are servants, and have their work assigned them.* Two kinds are here mentioned. (1) Stewards. These seem to be the servants to whom he gave authority. All ministers should be stewards—rightly dividing the Word of life—giving to every one of the family his portion of meat in due season. Oh! it is a blessed work, to feed the Church of God, which he hath purchased with his own blood—to give milk to babes, and strong meat to grown men— to give convenient food to every one. Pray for your ministers, that they may be made faithful and wise stewards. There are few such. (2) Porters. He commanded the porter to watch. It is the office of some ministers to stand at the door and invite every sinner, saying: "Enter ye in at the strait gate." Some ministers have not the gift of feeding the Church of God and watering it. Paul planted —Apollos watered. Some are only door-keepers in the house of my God. Learn not to despise any of the true servants of God. Are all apostles? Are all prophets? He has appointed some to stand at the door, and some to break the children's bread—despise neither.

2. *All Christians are servants, and have their work assigned them.* Some people think that ministers only have to work for Christ; but see here: "He gave to every man his work." In a great house, the steward and the porter are not the only servants; there are many more, and all have their work to do. Just so among the people of Christ. Ministers are not the only servants of Christ; all that believe on him are his servants.

(1) Learn to be working Christians. "Be ye doers of the Word, and not hearers only, deceiving your own souls." It is very striking

68

to see the uselessness of many Christians. Are there none of you who know what it is to be selfish in your Christianity ? You have seen a selfish child go into a secret place to enjoy some delicious morsels undisturbed by his companions ? So it is with some Christians. They feed upon Christ and forgiveness; but it is alone, and all for themselves. Are there not some of you who can enjoy being a Christian, while your dearest friend is not; and yet you will not speak to him ? See here, you have got your work to do. When Christ found you, he said: " Go, work in my vineyard." What were you hired for, if it was not to work ? What were you saved for, if it was not to spread salvation ? What blessed for ? Oh ! my Christian friends ! how little you live as if you were servants of Christ !—how much idle time and idle talk you have ! This is not like a good servant. How many things you have to do for yourself ! —how few for Christ and his people ! This is not like a servant.

(2) Learn to keep to your own work. In a great house every servant has his own peculiar work. One man is the porter to open the door; another is the steward to provide food for the family; a third has to clean the rooms; a fourth has to dress the food; a fifth has to wait upon the guests. Every one has his proper place, and no servant interferes with another. If all were to become porters, and open the door, then what would become of the stewardship ? or, if all were to be stewards, who would clean the house ? Just so is it with Christians. Every one has his peculiar work assigned him, and should not leave it. " Let every man abide in the same calling wherein he was called." Obadiah had his work appointed him in the court of the wicked Ahab. God placed him as his servant there, saying: " Work here for me." Does any of you belong to a wicked family ? Seek not to be removed—Christ has placed you there to be his servant—work for him. The Shunammite had her work. When the prophet asked: " Wilt thou be spoken for to the king ?" she said: " I dwell among mine own people." Once a poor demoniac whom Jesus healed, besought Jesus that he might follow after him; how-beit Jesus suffered him not, but saith unto him: " Go home to thy friends, and tell them how great things the Lord hath done for thee, and how he hath had compassion on thee." Learn, my dear friends,

to keep to your own work. When the Lord has hung up a lamp in one corner, is there no presumption in removing it to another? Is not the Lord wiser than man? Every one of you have your work to do for Christ *where you are.* Are you on a sick-bed? Still you have your work to do for Christ there as much as the highest servant of Christ in the world. The smallest twinkling star is as much a servant of God as the mid-day sun. Only live for Christ where you are.

IV. *Christ is coming back again, and we know not when:* "Watch ye therefore: for ye know not when the master of the house cometh, at even, or at midnight, or at the cockcrowing, or in the morning: lest, coming suddenly, he find you sleeping. (Verses 35, 36.) Two things are here declared.

1. *That Christ is coming back again.* The whole Bible bears witness to this. The master of the house has been a long time away on his journey; but he will come back again. When Christ ascended from his disciples, and a cloud received him out of their sight, and they were looking stedfastly into heaven, the angels said: "Ye men of Galilee, why stand ye gazing up into heaven? This same Jesus which is taken up from you into heaven, shall so come in like manner as ye have seen him go into heaven." He went up in a cloud—he shall come in the clouds.

2. *That Christ will come back suddenly.* The whole Bible bears witness to this. (1) In one place it is compared to a snare which suddenly entraps the unwary wild beast: "As a snare shall it come on all them that dwell on the face of the whole earth." (2) Again, to a thief: "The day of the Lord so cometh as a thief in the night." (3) Again, to a bridegroom coming suddenly: "At midnight there was a cry made, Behold the bridegroom cometh." (4) Again, to the waters of the flood. (5) Again, to the fiery rain that fell on Sodom and Gomorrah. (6) And here to the sudden coming home of the master of the house: "Ye know not when the master of the house cometh." Now, my dear friends, I am far from discouraging those who, with humble prayerfulness, search into the records of prophecy to find out what God has said as to the second coming of the Son of

Man. We are not like the first disciples of Jesus, if we do not often put the question: " What shall be the sign of thy coming, and of the end of the world ? " But the truth which I wish to be written on your hearts is this: That the coming shall be sudden—sudden to the world—sudden to the children of God: " In such an hour as ye think not, the Son of Man cometh." " Ye know not when the master of the house cometh, at even, or at midnight, or at cockcrowing, or in the morning." Oh, my friends ! your faith is incomplete, if you do not live in the daily faith of a coming Saviour.

V. *Watch:* " And what I say unto you I say unto all, Watch." (Verse 37.)

1. *Ministers should watch.* This word is especially addressed to the porter: " Watch ye, therefore." Ah ! how watchful we should be. Many things make us sleep. (1) Want of faith. When a minister loses sight of Christ crucified—risen—coming again—then he cannot watch for souls. Pray that your ministers may have a watching eye always on Christ. (2) Seeing so many careless souls. Ah ! you little know how this staggers the ministers of Christ. A young believer comes with a glowing heart to tell of Christ, and pardon, and the new heart. He knows it is the truth of God—he states it simply, freely, with all his heart—he presses it on men—he hopes to see them melt like icicles before the sun—alas ! they are as cold and dead as ever. They live on in their sins—they die in their sins. Ah ! you little know how this makes him dull, and heavy, and heart-broken. My friends, pray that we may not sleep. Pray that your carelessness may only make us watch the more.

2. *Christians should watch.* Ah ! if Christ is at hand, (1) Take heed lest you be found unforgiven. Many Christians seem to live without a realizing view of Christ. The eye should be fixed on Christ. Your eye is shut. Oh ! if you would abide in Christ, then let him come to-night—at even, or at midnight, or at cockcrow, or in the morning—he is welcome, thrice welcome ! Even so, come, Lord Jesus. (2) Take heed lest you be found in any course of sin. Many Christians seem to walk, if I mistake not, in courses of sin. It is hard to account for it; but so it seems to be. Some Christians seem

71

to be sleeping—in luxury—in covetousness—in evil company. Ah! think how would you like to be overtaken thus by the coming Saviour. Try your daily occupations—your daily state of feeling—your daily enjoyments—try them by this test: Am I doing as I would wish to do on the day of his coming?

3. Christless souls, how dreadful is your case! Death may be sudden—oh! how awfully sudden it sometimes is. You may have no time for repentance—no breath to pray! The coming of the Saviour shall be more sudden still. Ye know neither the day nor the hour. You know not God—you have not obeyed the Gospel. Oh! what will ye do in the day of the Lord's anger?

LOT'S WIFE

" But his wife looked back from behind him and she became a pillar of salt."—GEN. xix. 26.

THERE is not in the whole Bible a more instructive history than that of Lot and his family. His own history shows well how the righteous scarcely are saved. His sons-in-law show well the way in which the Gospel is received by the easy, careless world. His wife is a type of those who are convinced, yet never converted—who flee from the wrath to come, yet perish after all; whilst the angels' laying hold on the lingering family, is a type of the gracious violence and sovereign mercy which God uses in delivering souls.

At present I mean to direct your thoughts to the case of Lot's wife, and to show the following.

Doctrine.—Many souls who have been awakened to flee from wrath, look behind, and are lost.

I. *Many flee, under terrors of natural conscience; but when these subside, they look back, and are lost.*

72

So it was with Lot's wife. She was not like the men of Sodom—intent upon the world and sin—quite unconcerned about their souls. She was not like her sons-in-law—she did not think her husband mocking—she was really alarmed, and really fled; and yet her terrors were like the morning cloud and the early dew, which quickly pass away. When the angels had brought them out of the gates of Sodom, they said: " Escape for thy life, look not behind thee; neither stay thou in all the plain; escape to the mountain, lest thou be consumed." And as long as these dreadful words were ringing in her ears, doubtless she fled with anxious footstep. The dreadful scene of the past night—the darkness—the anxiety of her husband—the pressing urgency of the noble angels—all conspired to awaken her natural conscience, and to make her flee. But now the hellish roar of the wicked Sodomites had ceased—the sun was already gilding the horizon, promising a glorious dawn—the plain of Jordan began to smile, well watered everywhere, as the garden of the Lord. Her sons-in-law—her friends—her house—her goods—her treasure—were still in Sodom; so her heart was there also. Her anxieties began to vanish with the darkness—she determined to take one look, to see if it was really destroyed—she " looked back from behind him, and became a pillar of salt."

So is it with many among us. Many flee under terrors of natural conscience, but when these subside, they look back, and are lost.

Some people pass through the world without any terrors of conscience—without any awakening or anxiety about their souls. (1) Some are like the men of Sodom, intent upon buying and selling—building and planting—marrying and giving in marriage; or they are greedy upon their lusts, and they have no ears to hear the sounds of coming wrath. As a man working hard at the anvil hears no noise from without, because of the noise of his own hammer; so these men hear nothing of coming vengeance, they are so busy with the work of their hands. (2) Some are like the sons-in-law of Lot. Yon shrewd, intelligent man of business thinks that ministers do but jest. We seem to them as one that mocks. They are so accustomed to see behind the scenes in other professions, that they think there must be deceit with us too. And when they can point to an insincere, ungodly minister, then their triumph is complete. These shrewd men think that ministers put serious words into their mouths, as other men put on suits of solemn black at funerals, just to look well, and to agree with the occasion. They think that ministers put frightful things into sermons just to frighten weak people, and to make the crowd wonder. Now these shrewd men are seldom, if ever, visited with terrors of conscience. They slip easily through the world into an undone eternity. (3) Some, again, slumber all their days under a worldly ministry. When God, in judgment, takes away the pure preaching of the Word, and sends a famine of the bread and water of life, their souls grow up quite hard and un-awakened. They grow proud, and cannot bear to hear the preaching of Christ—they stop their ears and run—they hate, they detest it. These souls often pass through life without the least awakening, and never know, till they are in hell, that they are lost souls. (4) But many worldly people have a season of anxiety about their soul. A dangerous illness, or some awful bereavement, or some threatening cloud of Providence, stirs them up to flee from the wrath to come. They are quite in earnest—they lay by their sins, and avoid their sinful companions, and apply diligently to the Bible, and attempt to pray, and seem to be really fleeing out of Sodom; but they dure only for a while—their concern is like the morning cloud and the early dew—it quickly passes away. The sun of prosperity begins to rise—their fears begin to vanish—they look behind, and are lost.

Are there none here who can look back on such a course as this? You remember when some providence awakened you to deepest seriousness—some sickness, or the approach of the pestilence, or some fearful dealing of God with your family, or the approach of a sacra-ment, made you anxiously flee out of Sodom. O how different you were from the gay, laughing, unconcerned world! You did not think ministers were mocking then. You read your Bible, and went down on your knees to pray very earnestly. But the storm blew over—the sun began to rise, and everything around you began to smile. You began to think it hard to leave all your friends—your sins—your worldly enjoyments—and that perhaps the wrath of God would not come down. You looked back, and this day you are as hard and immovable as a pillar of salt. "Remember Lot's wife."

Learn two things:—

1. That an awakening by mere natural conscience is very different from an awakening by the Spirit of God. No man ever fled to Christ from mere natural terror. "No man can come to me," saith Christ, "except the Father which hath sent me draw him." Seek a divine work upon your heart.

2. Learn how far you are from the kingdom of God. You are quite lost. You are unmoved and unaffected by all we can say. You do not weep—you do not beat upon the breast—you do not flee, though we can prove to you that you are lying under the wrath of the great God that made you. Yet you do not stir one step to flee. Oh! how like you are to the pillar of salt—how likely it is that you will never be saved.

II. *Many flee when their friends are fleeing; but they look back, and are lost.*

So it was with Lot's wife. Of all the things which helped to awaken that unfortunate woman, I doubt not the most powerful was the anxiety of her husband. If he had not been anxious, I doubt not she would have been as stupid and unconcerned as her neighbours around her. But when she looked upon the anxious countenance of her beloved lord—when she saw how serious and earnest he was in pleading with their sons-in-law, then she could not but share in his anxiety. She had partaken of all his trials, of all his prosperities, and of all his troubles, and she would not leave him now. She clave unto him—she laid hold on the skirt of his garment, determined to be saved, or to perish with her husband. So much for the amiable and interesting affections of nature; but nature is not grace—natural affection carried her out of Sodom, but it did not carry her into Zoar; for she looked behind him, and became a pillar of salt.

Now, there is reason to think that this is true of some in this congregation—that they flee when their friends are fleeing, but look back, and are lost.

Nothing is more powerful in awakening souls than the example of others awakened to flee. It was so in the case of Ruth, when she clave to Naomi, saying: " Where thou goest I will go." It was so in the case of the daughters of Jerusalem, when they saw the bride in anxious search of her beloved: " Whither is thy beloved gone, that we may seek him with thee ? " It is foretold that it shall be so in the latter day, when " ten men shall lay hold on the skirt of him that is a Jew, saying: We will go with you; for we have heard that God is with you." It was so in the time of John the Baptist, when many of the Pharisees and Sadducees came to be baptized, and John said: " O generation of vipers, who hath warned you to flee from the wrath to come ? "

There is something very moving in the sight of some beloved one going to join the peculiar people of God. When he begins to flee from his old haunts of pleasure—no longer to laugh at wicked jests— no longer to delight in sinful company—when he becomes a reader of the Bible, and prays with earnestness, and waits with anxiety on the preached Word—it is a very moving sight to all his friends. No doubt, some are made bitter against him; for Christ came to set the daughter against her mother, and the daughter-in-law against her mother-in-law; but some are awakened to flee along with him.

Are there none here who were moved to flee because some dear friend was fleeing ? " Is there no wife that was awakened to flee with her husband, but grew weary and looked back, and is now become like Lot's wife ? Is there none here that was made truly anxious by seeing some companions anxious about their soul ? They wept, and you could not but weep; they felt themselves lost; and you, for the time, felt along with them. They were very eager in their inquiries after a Saviour, and you joined them in their eagerness. And where is all your anxiety now ? It is gone, like the morning cloud and early dew. You looked behind, and are now unmoved as a pillar of salt.

It was quite right to flee with them—it was right to cleave to them; for if not, you would certainly be hardened; if you stand out such moving invitations, nothing else will persuade you. If it was right to flee, it is right to flee still. Why should you look back ?

They are going to be blessed, and will you not go with them ? They are fleeing from wrath, and will you not flee with them ? " Remember Lot's wife." Have you made up your mind to separate eternally ? If not, why then have you let them go ? Why have you given up the first good movement in your breast ? Flee still—cleave to them, and say: " We will go with you."

II. *Some are laid hold of by God, and made to flee, who yet look back, and are lost.*

So it was with Lot's wife. Not only were natural means made use of to make her flee, but supernatural means also. Not only was she moved by sudden terror, and by the example of her husband, but she was drawn out by the angels: " And while he lingered, the men laid hold upon his hand, and upon the hand of his wife, and upon the hand of his two daughters; the Lord being merciful unto him: and they brought him forth, and set him without the city." (Verse 16.) She shared in the same divine help as her husband—God was merciful to her as he was to her husband. The same mighty hand was put forth to save her, and actually plucked her as a brand out of the burning; but, observe, the same hand did not pull her into Zoar, nor lift her away to the cave of the mountain. . Grace did something for her, but it did not do everything. She looked back, and became a pillar of salt.

So is it, we fear, with some among us. Some seem to be laid hold of by God, and made to flee, who yet look back, and are lost. Now, there are a great many among us of whom we have no right to say or to think that they have ever been laid hold of by God.

1. There are many among us who seem to live in utter ignorance of their lost condition—who plead the innocence of their lives even when Death is laying his cold hand upon them. There are some poor souls who seem to die willing to be judged by the law. I have lived a decent life, they will say; I have been a harmless, quiet-living man; and I can see no reason why the wrath of the great God should ever come upon me. Oh ! brethren, if this is your case, it is very plain that you have never had a divine awakening. The power of God alone could awaken you to flee.

2. There are many among us who live in the daily practice of sin—some who carry on small dishonesties, or occasionally use minced oaths—who walk in the counsel of the ungodly. O brethren! if this be your case, it is quite plain that you have never had a divine awakening. When a man is made anxious about his soul, he always puts away his open sins.

3. There are many among us who live much in the neglect of the means of grace—some who very seldom read the Bible when alone, or never but on Sabbath-days—some who do not pray regularly, nor with any earnestness—some who are very careless about the house of God, contented if they attend it only once on the Sabbath-day—who make no conscience of being up betimes, and ready for the house of God in the morning—who allow the silliest excuses to keep them away—who loiter about on the Sabbath-day—who devote it to most unhallowed visiting, or walking in the fields—making it the most unholy day in the week. Oh! dear souls, if this be your case, then it is quite plain you have never been laid hold on by God. You are as dead and unawakened as the stones you walk upon. You are living in the very heart of Sodom, and the wrath of God abideth on you.

But there are some among us of whom we think that they have been laid hold on by God, and made to flee. There are some who show evident marks that God has been making them flee out of Sodom. The marks are these:—

1. They have a deep sense of their lost condition; they have an abiding conviction that the time past of their lives has been spent under the wrath of the great God that made them; their concern goes with them wherever they go; and anxiety is painted on their very countenance. Is this your condition? Then you have indeed been awakened by God.

2. They dare not go back to their open sins—they break off quite suddenly from their little dishonesties, their swearing, or evil-speaking—they separate from their wicked companions and filthy conversation—they feel that death is in the cup, and they dare not drink it any longer. Is this your case? Then there is reason to think you have been awakened by God.

78

3. They are anxious users of the means of grace. They search the Scriptures night and day—they pray with earnestness—they are unwearied in waiting on ordinances—suffer no trifle to keep them away from the house of God—they seek for the Saviour as for hid treasure—listen for his name as the criminal for the sound of pardon. Is this your case ? Then it seems likely that God has been merciful to your soul—that God has been making you flee out of Sodom, and escape for your life.

But the text shows me that many who have been thus awakened look back, and are lost. "Remember Lot's wife." She was brought quite out of Sodom, and yet she looked back, and became a pillar of salt. She was awakened, yet never saved. Now, there is reason to fear this may be the case with some amongst us. (1) Some awakened souls begin to despair of ever finding Christ. They begin to blame God for not having brought them into peace before now; and so they give up striving to enter in at the strait gate—they look behind, and are lost. (2) Some awakened souls begin to think themselves saved already. They have put away many outward sins, and prayed with much earnestness. Their friends observe the change, and they think they are surely safe now—that there is no need of fleeing any farther; so they look behind, and become a pillar of salt. (3) Some awakened souls begin to tire of the pains of seeking Christ. They remember their former ease and pleasures—their companions —their walks—their merry-makings; so they look behind, and perish.

Speak a word to awakened souls. Some now hearing me may be at present under the awakening hand of God. You have deep convictions of your lost condition, you have put away outward sins, and wait earnestly on every means of grace—there is every reason to think that God has been merciful to you, and has laid hold upon you. "Remember Lot's wife."

Learn from her (1) That you are not saved yet. Lot's wife fled out of Sodom, led by the angel's hand, and yet she was lost. An awakened soul is not a saved soul. You are not saved till God shut you into Christ. It is not enough that you flee—you must flee into Christ. Oh ! do not lie down and slumber. Oh ! do not look behind you. " Remember Lot's wife." (2) That God is no ways obliged to bring you into Christ. God has made but one covenant—that is, with Christ and all in him; but he has nowhere bound himself to men that are out of Christ. He may never bring you to Christ, and yet be a just and righteous God. Do not demand it of God, then, as if he were obliged to save you, but lie helpless at his feet as a sovereign God.

Speak a word to those who are beginning to look back. There is reason to think that some who were once awakened by God have begun to look back. (1) Some of you have begun to lose a sense of your wretched and lost condition. Some of you have quite another view of your state from what you had. (2) Some of you have gone back to old sins—to old habits, especially of keeping company with the ungodly; and some, there is reason to think, are trying to laugh at their former fears. (3) Some of you have turned more careless of the Bible, and of prayer, and of the ordinances. At last sacrament there were many very eager to hear of Christ; and where are they now ? There is reason to fear that much of that concern is gone— that many have lost their anxiety—that some are looking back.

Now, " remember Lot's wife." (1) It will not save you, that you were once anxious—nay, that you were made anxious by God. So was Lot's wife, and yet she was lost. (2) If you really look back, it is probable you never will be awakened again. Consider that monument of vengeance on the Plain of Jordan—speak to her, she does not hear—cry, she does not regard you—urge her to flee again from wrath, she does not move—she is dead. So will it be with you. If you really turn back now, we may speak, but you will not hear— we may cry, but you will not regard—we may urge you again to flee, but you will not move. " If any man draw back, my soul shall have no pleasure in him "—" No man, having put his hand to the plough, and looking back, is fit for the kingdom of God."

WILL YE ALSO GO AWAY?

" From that time many of his disciples went back, and walked no more
with him. Then said Jesus unto the twelve, Will ye also go away ?
Then Simon Peter answered him, Lord, to whom shall we go ?
thou hast the words of eternal life. And we believe and are sure that
thou art that Christ, the Son of the living God."—JOHN vi. 66–69.

WE will consider three lessons brought before us here.

I. Lesson. *Many who seem to be disciples of Christ, go back, and
walk no more with Jesus.*

This is a very solemn truth, and may probably answer the case
of some who are this day hearing me. Observe, it is said twice over
that there were many who went back. If there were many then,
it is likely there will be many now.

1. *Many follow Christ for a time, but are stumbled when they hear
they must come to personal union with Christ.*

(1) So it was here. A great many were now following Christ in
addition to the twelve apostles. They were evidently much taken
with Christ; they called him a prophet; they wanted to make him
a king; they followed him across the sea; and yet, when he told them
that he was the bread of heaven, they murmured—when he told
them that they must eat his flesh and drink his blood to have eternal
life, they said: " This is a hard saying;" and it was for this reason
they turned back, and walked no more with Jesus.

(2) So it is now. A great many persons are much taken with
Christ; they have some anxiety about their souls; they follow
anxiously after the preaching of the Word; but when we show them
that Christ is the bread of heaven—that they must have a personal
closing with Christ, as much as if they were to eat his flesh and drink
his blood—these souls say: " It is a hard saying, who can hear it ? "
By and by, they are offended—they believe not—they go back, and
walk no more with Jesus. Is any of you who are hearing me in this
condition ? Oh ! think again, I beseech you, before you go back.

81

Oh! seek the teaching of God, and he will show you that none of Christ's sayings are hard sayings, but that they are all sweet and easy. When the heart of a poor Indian was brought under the teaching of God, he said: "Some people complain that the Bible is a hard book; but I have not read so far as to find it a hard book. To me it is all sweet and easy."

2. *Many follow Christ for a time, but when they are told that Christ must dwell in them, they go back, and walk no more with Jesus.*

(1) So it was here. The multitude that followed Christ were pleased with a great many things in him. When he fed them with the five barley loaves and the two fishes, they said: "Lord, it is good for us to be here"—"This is in truth that prophet that should come into the world." And again, when Jesus told them of bread from heaven that would give life, they said most devoutly: "Lord, evermore give us this bread." But, when Christ said: "He that eateth my flesh, and drinketh my blood, dwelleth in me, and I in him," by and by they were offended. When he told them that he would be their life, and would dwell in them, they said: "It is a hard saying, who can hear it?" They believed not—they went back, and walked no more with Jesus.

(2) So it was in some measure with Nicodemus. When he regarded Christ as a worker of miracles, this drew the heart of the Jewish ruler, and he said to him: "Rabbi, we know thou art a teacher come from God." But when Jesus told him that he must be born again—must be indwelt by the unseen Spirit of God— Nicodemus found it a hard saying: "How can a man be born when he is old?" And again: "How can these things be?"

(3) So now, many persons are much taken with Christ. They are anxious about their souls for a time: and they see some glimpses of Christ as a Saviour. They love to hear the Word; "it is like a very lovely song of one that hath a pleasant voice, and can play well on an instrument;" but when Christ says: "Ye must be born again" —"He that eateth me, even he shall live by me"—they say: "This is a hard saying, who can hear it?" 1*st*, They never saw the Spirit, and they say: "How can these things be?" This is one of your mysteries. Therefore, they go back, and walk no more with Jesus.

Is any hearing me in this condition ? Oh ! think a moment before you go back: " Oh ! fools, and slow of heart to believe all that is written concerning Jesus." Why should you stumble at the blessed word: " He that eateth me shall live by me ? " True, you never saw the Spirit; yet trust the word of him that cannot lie. You never saw the wind, and yet you spread the sail; so trust to that Spirit, though you never saw him. *2nd*, Some of you may fear that if it be true, then you would be deprived of some of your darling pleasures—your heart would be changed, and you would no more have a relish for your present enjoyments; therefore you go back, and walk no more with Jesus. Oh ! how the devil blinds your understanding. Do you not see, that if you lose your relish for your present joys, it will be because you have got a taste for higher and sweeter ? You might as wisely refuse to drink better wine, because you would thereby lose your relish for the worse. Oh ! the joys of the Holy Ghost are sweeter than all the pleasures of sin. It is wine on the lees, well refined. " Woe unto thee, O Jerusalem ! wilt thou not be made clean ? When shall it once be ? "

3. *Many are awakened to follow Christ, but when they find that they must be drawn to Christ—that all is of free grace—by-and-by they are offended.*

(1) So here, the persons that had followed Christ had been laborious and painstaking in following him—they had crossed the sea, and listened to his words for many days together; and doubtless they began to think they had done well, and that they were worthy to be saved for the pains they had taken. But when Jesus told them that salvation was of mere grace—that they were helpless sinners, and needed still to be drawn to Christ by the mere good pleasure of the Father—this offended them to the quick—they turned back, and walked no more with Jesus.

(2) So now, many persons set out in religion, thinking that they shall soon bring themselves into a converted state. They take great pains in religion; they confess the sins of their past life, and stir up grief in their hearts because of them; they wait patiently on ordinances, and take much pains to work the works of God: but when they find out that they are not a whit nearer being saved than when

they began—when they are told they must be drawn to Christ—that God is not obliged to save them—that they deserve nothing at his hand but a place in hell—that if ever they are saved, it is of mere free grace—then they are offended. They cannot bear this kind of preaching; they go back, and walk no more with Jesus. Is any hearing me in this condition ? Alas ! proud sinner, stop one moment before you leave the divine Saviour. Is it a hard saying, that an infinitely hateful rebel and worm should be unable to buy Christ with so many tears and prayers ?

Listen here to two words of warning:—

1st, Many go so far with Christ, who do not go the whole way. Many hear Christ's words for a time with joy and eagerness, who yet are offended by them at last. This is a solemn warning. Do not think you are a Christian because you sit and listen to the words of Christ. Do not think you are a Christian because you have some pleasure in the words of Christ. Many are called—few are chosen. Many went back, and only twelve remained. So doubtless it will be found among you. Those only are Christians who feed upon Christ, and live by him.

2nd, Those that go back generally walk no more with Jesus. Perhaps they did not intend to bid an eternal farewell to the Saviour. Perhaps they said as they retired, I will go home and think about it; I will hear him again concerning this matter. At a more convenient season I will follow him. But, alas ! that season never came—they walked no more with Jesus. Take warning, dear friends, you that are anxious about your souls. Oh ! do not be easily offended. Do not lose a sense of your lost condition. Oh ! do not grow careless of your Bible and the means of grace. Oh ! do not go back to the company of sinners. These are all marks of one who is going back from Jesus. Wait patiently for the Lord until he incline his ear and hear your cry. Still press to hear the words of Jesus. Still cry for the teaching Spirit. " If any man draw back, my soul shall have no pleasure in him "—" No man having put his hand to the plough, and looking back, is fit for the kingdom of God."

II. Lesson. *The careful anxiety of Christ lest his own true disciples should go away:* " Then said Jesus to the twelve, Will ye also go away ? " (Verse 67.)

I have no doubt the heart of Jesus was grieved when the multitude went away, and walked no more with him. That good Shepherd never yet saw a lost sheep running on to destruction, but his heart bled for it: " O Jerusalem, Jerusalem, how often would I have gathered thy children together ! " He could see all the future history of these men—how they would lose all their impressions—how they would harden in their sins— now, like a rolling snowball, they would gather more and more wrath around them, and I doubt not, he wept in secret over them, and said: " If ye had known, even you, the things which belong unto your peace; but now they are hid from your eyes." He traced their history up to that hour when he would say: " Depart from me." But however much Christ grieved over their departure, this only fanned the flame of his love to his own, so that he turned round and said: " Will ye also go away ? "

1. Observe how much love there is in these words. When the crowd went away he did not cry after them—his soul was grieved, but he spoke not a word; but when his own believing disciples were in danger of being led away, he speaks to them: " Will ye also go away ? "—ye whom I have chosen—ye whom I have washed—ye whom I have sanctified and filled with hopes of glory—" Will ye also go, away ? " Oh ! see, Christians, how anxiously Christ watches over you. He is walking in the midst of the seven golden candlesticks, and his word is: " I know thy works." He watches the first decaying of the first love. He speaks aloud: " Will ye also go away ? "

2. Observe, Christ keeps his disciples from backsliding, by putting the question to them: " Will ye also go away ? " It is probable that some of the twelve were inclining to go away with the rest. We are often deceived by example—carried away from Christ before we think of it: but Christ wakens us by the question: " Will ye also go away ? " Think of this question, you that have known Christ, and yet are going back to sin and the world. May God write it on your hearts: " Will ye also go away ? " Christians, if you would

85

keep this word in your heart, it would keep you from the thought of going away.

III. Lesson. *A true believer has none to go to but Christ.*

Both the Bible and experience testify, that believers do oftentimes go away from Christ. The same lips that said: "My Lord, and my God," are often found saying: "I will go after my lovers." But this passage plainly shows that it needs but the word of the tender Saviour to reach the heart of the backslider, and he says: "Lord, to whom shall we go? thou hast the words of eternal life."

Two reasons are here given why the believer cleaves to Christ.

1. "Thou hast the words of eternal life." To unconverted minds the words of Christ are hard sayings; to his own, they are tried words —words of eternal life. The very thing that drives the world away from Christ, draws his own disciples closer and closer to him. The world are offended when Christ says we must eat his flesh—it is a word of eternal life to the Christian. The world go away when they hear of Christ dwelling in the soul—the Christian draws nearer, and says: Lord, evermore dwell in me. The world walk no more with Jesus when they hear, It is all of grace—the Christian bows in the dust, and blesses God, who alone has made him to differ: "Lord, to whom shall we go? thou hast the words of eternal life." Dear friends, try yourselves by this. Are the words of Christ to you hard sayings, or are they the words of eternal life? Oh! may God enable you to judge fairly of your case.

2. "We believe and are sure that thou art that Christ, the Son of the living God." Ah! it is this that rivets the believing soul to Christ—the certain conviction that Christ is a divine Saviour. If Christ were only a man like ourselves, then how could he be a surety for us? He might suffer in the stead of one man, but how could he suffer in the stead of thousands? Ah! but I believe and am sure that he is the Son of the living God, and therefore I know he is a sufficient surety for me. To whom else can I go for pardon? If Christ were only a man like ourselves, then how could he dwell in us, or give the Spirit to abide with us for ever? But we believe and are sure that he is that Christ, the Son of the living God, and therefore

we know he is able to dwell in us, and put the Spirit in us for ever. To whom, then, can I go for a new heart but unto Christ ? O dear brethren ! have you been thus taught ?—then blessed are ye; " for flesh and blood hath not revealed it unto you, but my Father which is in heaven." Hold fast by this sure faith—you cannot be too sure, and then you will never, never go away from Christ.

Some of you are very wavering in your life, like a wave of the sea, driven with the wind and tossed; at one time cast upon the shore, at another time running back into the sea. There is no decision about your Christianity or about your holiness. Why is this ? It is unbelief. Oh ! if you would believe and be sure, then you would never depart from him. You would say: " To whom shall we go ? because thou hast the words of eternal life."

CONVICTION OF SIN

" And when he [the Comforter] is come, he will convince the world of sin, and of righteousness, and of judgment."—JOHN xvi. 8.

WHEN friends are about to part from one another, they are far kinder than ever they have been before. It was so with Jesus. He was going to part from his disciples, and never till now did his heart flow out toward them in so many streams of heavenly tenderness. Sorrow had filled their heart, and therefore divinest compassion filled his heart. " I tell you the truth, it is expedient for you that I go away."

Surely it was expedient for himself that he should go away. He had lived a life of weariness and painfulness, not having where to lay his head, and surely it was pleasant in his eyes that he was about to enter into his rest. He had lived in obscurity and poverty—he

87

gave his back to the smiters, and his cheeks to them that plucked off the hair; and now, surely, he might well look forward with joy to his return to that glory which he had with the Father before ever the world was, when all the angels of God worshipped him; and yet he does not say: It is expedient for me that I go away. Surely that would have been comfort enough to his disciples. But no; he says: " It is expedient for you." He forgets himself altogether, and thinks only of his little flock which he was leaving behind him: " It is expedient for you that I go away." O most generous of Saviours ! He looked not on his own things, but on the things of others also. He knew that it is far more blessed to give than it is to receive.

The gift of the Spirit is the great argument by which he here persuades them that his going away would be expedient for them. Now, it is curious to remark that he had promised them the Spirit before, in the beginning of his discourse. In chap. xiv. 16-18, he says: " I will pray the Father, and he shall give you another Comforter, that he may abide with you for ever; even the Spirit of truth; whom the world cannot receive, because it seeth him not, neither knoweth him: but ye know him; for he dwelleth with you, and shall be in you. I will not leave you comfortless: I will come to you." And again: " But the Comforter, which is the Holy Ghost, whom the Father will send in my name, he shall teach you all things, and bring all things to your remembrance, whatsoever I have said unto you." (Verse 26.) In that passage he promises the Spirit for their own peculiar comfort and joy. He promises him as a treasure which they, and they only, could receive: " For the world cannot receive him, because it neither sees nor knows him;" and yet, saith he, " he dwelleth with you, and shall be in you." But in the passage before us the promise is quite different. He promises the Spirit here, not for themselves, but for the world—not as a peculiar treasure, to be locked up in their own bosoms, which they might brood over with a selfish joy, but as a blessed power to work, through their preaching, on the wicked world around them—not as a well springing up within their own bosoms unto everlasting life, but as rivers of living water flowing through them to water this dry and perishing world. He does not say: When he is come he will fill your hearts with peace and joy to overflowing; but: "When he is come, he will convince the world of sin, and of righteousness, and of judgment." But a little before he had told them that the world would hate and persecute them: "If ye were of the world, the world would love his own; but because ye are not of the world, but I have chosen you out of the world, therefore the world hateth you." (John xv. 19.) This was but poor comfort, when that very world was to be the field of their labours; but now he shows them what a blessed gift the Spirit would be; for he would work, through their preaching, upon the very hearts that hated and persecuted them: "He shall convince the world of sin." This has always been the case. In Acts ii. we are told that when the Spirit came on the apostles the crowd mocked them, saying: "These men are full of new wine;" and yet, when Peter preached, the Spirit wrought through his preaching on the hearts of these very scoffers. They were pricked in their hearts, and cried: "Men and brethren, what must we do?" and the same day three thousand souls were converted. Again, the jailer at Philippi was evidently a hard, cruel man towards the apostles; for he thrust them into the inner prison, and made their feet fast in the stocks; and yet the Spirit opens his hard heart, and he is brought to Christ by the very apostles whom he hated. Just so it is, brethren, to this day. The world do not love the true ministers of Christ a whit better than they did. The world is the same world that it was in Christ's day. That word has never yet been scored out of the Bible: "Whosoever will live godly in the world, must suffer persecution." We expect, as Paul did, to be hated by the most who listen to us. We are quite sure, as Paul was, that the more abundantly we love you, most of you will love us the less; and yet, brethren, none of these things move us. Though cast down, we are not in despair; for we know that the Spirit is sent to convince the world; and we do not fear but some of you who are counting us an enemy, because we tell you the truth, may even this day, in the midst of all your hatred and cold indifference, be convinced of sin by the Spirit, and made to cry out: "Sirs, what must I do to be saved?"

I. *The first work of the Spirit is to convince of sin.*

1. *Who it is that convinces of sin :* " He shall convince the world of sin, because they believe not in me." It is curious to remark, that wherever the Holy Ghost is spoken of in the Bible, he is spoken of in terms of gentleness and love. We often read of the wrath of God the Father, as in Rom. i.: " The wrath of God is revealed from heaven against all ungodliness and unrighteousness of men." And we often read of the wrath of God the Son: " Kiss the Son, lest he be angry, and ye perish from the way;" or, " Revealed from heaven taking vengeance." But we nowhere read of the wrath of God the Holy Ghost. He is compared to a dove, the gentlest of all creatures. He is warm and gentle as the breath: " Jesus breathed on them, and said, Receive ye the Holy Ghost." He is gentle as the falling dew: " I will be as the dew unto Israel." He is soft and gentle as oil; for he is called " The oil of gladness." The fine oil wherewith the high priest was anointed was a type of the Spirit. He is gentle and refreshing as the springing well: " The water that I shall give him shall be in him a well of water springing up unto everlasting life." He is called " The Spirit of grace and of supplications." He is nowhere called the Spirit of wrath. He is called the " Holy Ghost, which is the Comforter." Nowhere is he called the Avenger. We are told that he groans within the heart of a believer, " helping his infirmities;" so that he greatly helps the believer in prayer. We are told also of the love of the Spirit—nowhere of the wrath of the Spirit. We are told of his being grieved: " Grieve not the Holy Spirit;" of his being resisted: "Ye do always resist the Holy Ghost;" of his being quenched: " Quench not the Spirit." But these are all marks of gentleness and love. Nowhere will you find one mark of anger or of vengeance attributed to him; and yet, brethren, when this blessed Spirit begins his work of love, mark how he begins—he convinces of sin. Even he, all-wise, almighty, all-gentle and loving though he be, cannot persuade a poor sinful heart to embrace the Saviour, without first opening up his wounds, and convincing him that he is lost.

Now, brethren, I ask of you, Should not the faithful minister of Christ just do the very same ? Ah ! brethren, if the Spirit, whose very breath is all gentleness and love—whom Jesus hath sent into the world to bring men to eternal life—if he begins his work in every soul that is to be saved by convincing of sin, why should you blame the minister of Christ if he begins in the very same way ? Why should you say that we are harsh, and cruel, and severe, when we begin to deal with your souls by convincing you of sin ? " " Am I become your enemy, because I tell you the truth ? " When the surgeon comes to cure a corrupted wound—when he tears off the vile bandages which unskilful hands had wrapped around it—when he lays open the deepest recesses of your wound, and shows you all its venom and its virulence—do you call him cruel ? May not his hands be all the time the hands of gentleness and love ? Or, when a house is all on fire—when the flames are bursting out from every window—when some courageous man ventures to alarm the sleeping inmates—bursts through the barred door—tears aside the close-drawn curtains, and with eager hand shakes the sleeper—bids him awake and flee—a moment longer, and you may be lost—do you call him cruel ? or do you say this messenger of mercy spoke too loud—too plain ? Ah, no. " Skin for skin, all that a man hath will he give for his life." Why, then, brethren, will you blame the minister of Christ when he begins by convincing you of sin ? Think you that the wound of sin is less venomous or deadly than a wound in the flesh ? Think you the flames of hell are less hard to bear than the flames of earth ? The very Spirit of love begins by convincing you of sin; and are we less the messengers of love because we begin by doing the same thing ? Oh, then, do not say that we are become your enemy because we tell you the truth ?

II. *What is this conviction of sin ?* I would begin to show this by showing you what it is not.

1. *It is not the mere smiting of the natural conscience.* Although man be utterly fallen, yet God has left natural conscience behind in every heart, to speak for him. Some men, by continual sinning, sear even the conscience as with a hot iron, so that it becomes dead and past feeling; but most men have so much natural conscience remaining, that they cannot commit open sin without their conscience smiting them. When a man commits murder or theft, no eye may

have seen him, and yet conscience makes a coward of him. He trembles and is afraid—he feels that he has sinned, and he fears that God will take vengeance. Now, brethren, that is not the conviction of sin here spoken of—that is a natural work which takes place in every heart; but conviction of sin is a supernatural work of the Spirit of God. If you have had nothing more than the ordinary smiting of conscience, then you have never been convinced of sin.

2. *It is not any impression upon the imagination.* Sometimes, when men have committed great sin, they have awful impressions of God's vengeance made upon their imaginations. In the night-time they almost fancy they see the flames of hell burning beneath them; or they seem to hear doleful cries in their ears telling of coming woe; or they fancy they see the face of Jesus all clouded with anger; or they have terrible dreams, when they sleep, of coming vengeance. Now, this is not the conviction of sin which the Spirit gives. This is altogether a natural work upon the natural faculties, and not at all a supernatural work of the Spirit. If you have had nothing more than these imaginary terrors, you have had no work of the Spirit.

3. *It is not a mere head knowledge of what the Bible says against sin.* Many unconverted men read their Bibles, and have a clear knowledge that their case is laid down there. They are sensible men. They know very well that they are in sin, and they know just as well that the wages of sin is death. One man lives a swearer, and he reads the words, and understands them perfectly: " Swear not at all "— " The Lord will not hold him guiltless that taketh his name in vain." Another man lives in the lusts of the flesh, and he reads the Bible, and understands these words perfectly: " No unclean person hath any inheritance in the kingdom of Christ and of God." Another man lives in habitual forgetfulness of God—never thinks of God from sunrise to sunset, and yet he reads: " The wicked shall be turned into hell, and all the people that forget God." Now, in this way most unconverted men have a head knowledge of their sin, and of the wages of sin; yet, brethren, this is far from conviction of sin. This is a mere natural work in the head. Conviction of sin is a work upon the heart. If you have had nothing more than this head

knowledge that you are sinners, then you have never been convinced of sin.

4. *Conviction of sin is not to feel the loathsomeness of sin.* This is what a child of God feels. A child of God has seen the beauty and excellency of God, and therefore sin is loathsome in his eyes. But no unconverted person has seen the beauty and excellency of God; therefore, even the Spirit cannot make him feel the loathsomeness of sin. Just as when you leave a room that is brilliantly lighted, and go out into the darkness of the open air, the night looks very dark; so when a child of God has been within the veil—in the presence of his reconciled God—in full view of the Father of lights, dwelling in light inaccessible and full of glory—then, when he turns his eye inwards upon his own sinful bosom, sin appears very dark, very vile, and very loathsome. But an unconverted soul never has been in the presence of the reconciled God; and therefore sin cannot appear dark and loathsome in his eyes. Just as when you have tasted something very sweet and pleasant, when you come to taste other things, they appear very insipid and disagreeable; so when a child of God has tasted and seen that God is gracious, the taste of sin in his own heart becomes very nauseous and loathsome to him. But an unconverted soul never tasted the sweetness of God's love; he cannot, therefore, feel the vileness and loathsomeness of sin. This, then, is not the conviction of sin here spoken of.

What, then, is this conviction of sin ? *Ans.* It is a just sense of the dreadfulness of sin. It is not a mere knowledge that we have many sins, and that God's anger is revealed against them all; but it is a heart-feeling that we are under sin. Again: it is not a feeling of the loathsomeness of sin—that is felt only by the children of God; but it is a feeling of the dreadfulness of sin—of the dishonour it does to God, and of the wrath to which it exposes the soul. Oh, brethren ! conviction of sin is no slight natural work upon the heart. There is a great difference between knowing a thing and having a just sense of it. There is a great difference between knowing that vinegar is sour, and actually tasting and feeling that it is sour. There is a great difference between knowing that fire will burn us, and actually feeling the pain of being burned. Just in the same way, there is all the difference in the world between knowing the dreadfulness of your sins and feeling the dreadfulness of your sins. It is all in vain that you read your Bibles and hear us preach, unless the Spirit use the words to give sense and feeling to your dead hearts. The plainest words will not awaken you as long as you are in a natural condition. If we could prove to you, with the plainness of arithmetic, that the wrath of God is abiding on you and your children, still you would sit unmoved—you would go away and forget it before you reached your own door. Ah, brethren! he that made your heart can alone impress your heart. It is the Spirit that convinceth of sin.

1. *Learn the true power of the read and preached Word.* It is but an instrument in the hand of God. It has no power of itself, except to produce natural impressions. It is a hammer—but God must break your hearts with it. It is a fire—but God must kindle up your bosoms with it. Without him we may give you a knowledge of the dreadfulness of your condition, but he only can give you a just sense and feeling of the dreadfulness of your condition. The most powerful sermon in the world can make nothing more than a natural impression; but when God works through it, the feeblest word makes a supernatural impression. Many a poor sermon has been the means by which God hath converted a soul. Children of God, O that you would pray night and day for the lifting up of the arm of God !

2. *Learn that conversion is not in your own power.* It is the Spirit alone who convinces of sin, and he is a free agent. He is a sovereign Spirit, and has nowhere promised to work at the bidding of unconverted men. He hath many on whom he will have mercy; and whom he will he hardeneth. Perhaps you think you may take your fill of sin just now, and then come and repent, and be saved; but remember the Spirit is not at your bidding. He is not your servant. Many hope to be converted on their death-bed; and they come to their death-bed, and yet are not converted. If the Spirit be working with you now, do not grieve him—do not resist him—do not quench him; for he may never come back to you again.

94

III. *I come to the argument which the Spirit uses.* There are two arguments by which the Spirit usually gives men a sense of the dreadfulness of sin.

1. *The Law:* " The law is our schoolmaster to bring us to Christ " —" Now we know that what things soever the law saith, it saith to them that are under the law, that every mouth may be stopped, and all the world become guilty before God." The sinner reads the law of the great God who made heaven and earth. The Spirit of God arouses his conscience to see that the law condemns every part of his life. The law bids him love God. His heart tells him he never loved God—never had a thought of regard toward God. The Spirit convinces him that God is a jealous God—that his honour is concerned to uphold the law, and destroy the sinner. The Spirit convinces him that God is a just God—that he can by no means clear the guilty. The Spirit convinces him that he is a true God— that he must fulfil all his threatenings: " Have I said it, and shall I not do it ? " The sinner's mouth is stopped, and he stands guilty before God.

2. *The second argument is the Gospel:* " Because they believe not on Jesus." This is the strongest of all arguments, and therefore is chosen by Christ here. The sinner reads in the Word that " he that believeth on the Son hath everlasting life;" and now the Spirit convinces him that he never believed on the Son of God— indeed, he does not know what it means. For the first time the conviction comes upon his heart: " He that believeth not the Son, shall not see life; but the wrath of God abideth on him." The more glorious and divine that Saviour is, the more is the Christless soul convinced that he is lost; for he feels that he is out of that Saviour. He sees plainly that Christ is an almighty ark riding over the deluge of God's wrath—he sees how safe and happy the little company are that are gathered within; but this just makes him gnash his teeth in agony, for he is not within the ark, and the waves and billows are coming over him. He hears that Christ hath been stretching out the hands all the day to the chief of sinners, not willing that any should perish; but then he never cast himself into these arms, and now he feels that Christ may be laughing at his calamity, and

mocking when his fear cometh. O yes, my friends! how often on the death-bed, when the natural fears of conscience are aided by the Spirit of God—how often, when we speak of Christ—his love—his atoning blood—the refuge to be found in him—how safe and happy all ere that are in him—how often does the dying sinner turn it all away with the awful question: *But am I in Christ?* The more we tell of the Saviour, the more is their agony increased; for they feel that that is the Saviour they have refused. Ah! what a meaning does that give to these words: " The Spirit convinceth of sin, because they believe not on me."

1. Now, my friends, there are many of you who know that you never believed on Jesus, and yet you are quite unmoved. You sit without any emotion—you eat your meals with appetite, and doubtless sleep sound at night. Do you wish to know the reason? You have never been convinced of sin. The Spirit hath never begun his work in your heart. Oh! if the Spirit of Jesus would come on your hearts like a mighty rushing wind, what a dreadful thought it would be to you this night, that you are lying out of Christ! You would lose your appetite for this world's food—you would not be able to rest in your bed—you would not dare to live on in your sins. All your past sins would rise behind you like apparitions of evil. Wherever you went you would meet the word: "Without Christ, without hope, and without God in the world;" and if your worldly friends should try to hush your fears, and tell you of your decencies, and that you were not so bad as your neighbours, and that many might fear if you feared, ah! how you would thrust them away, and stop your ears, and cry: There is a city of refuge, to which I have never fled; therefore there must be a blood-avenger. There is an ark; therefore there must be a coming deluge. There is a Christ; therefore there must be a hell for the Christless.

2. Some of you may be under conviction of sin—you feel the dreadfulness of being out of Christ, and you are very miserable. Now, (1) Be thankful for this work of the Spirit: " Flesh and blood hath not revealed it unto thee, but my Father." God hath brought you into the wilderness just that he might allure you, and speak to your heart about Christ. This is the way he begins the work in

every soul he saves. Nobody ever came to Christ but they were first convinced of sin. All that are now in heaven began this way. Be thankful you are not dead like those around you. (2) Do not lose these convictions. Remember they are easily lost. Involve yourself over head and ears in business, and work even on the Sabbath-day, and you will soon drive all away. Indulge a little in sensual pleasure—take a little diversion with companions, and you will soon be as happy and careless as they. If you love your soul, flee these things—do not stay—flee away from them. Read the books that keep up your anxiety—wait on the ministers that keep up that anxiety. Above all, cry to the Spirit, who alone was the author of it, that he would keep it up. Cry night and day that he may never let you rest out of Christ. Oh! would you sleep over hell? (3) Do not rest in these convictions. You are not saved yet. Many have come thus far and perished after all—many have been convinced, not converted—many lose their convictions, and wallow in sin again. "Remember Lot's wife." You are never safe till you are within the fold. Christ is the door. "Strive to enter in at the strait gate; for many shall seek to enter in and shall not be able."

Dundee, Feb. 4, 1837.

CONVICTION OF RIGHTEOUSNESS

"And when he [the Comforter] is come, he will convince the world of sin, and of righteousness, and of judgment."—JOHN xvi. 8.

IN my last discourse from this passage we saw that the first work of the Spirit on the heart of a sinner is to convince of sin—to give him a sense of the dreadfulness of his sins, and to make him feel how surely he is a lost sinner. And from that I drew an argument, that it is the duty of all faithful ministers to do the same; that if the Spirit of gentleness and love begins his work on the soul by awakening in it a deep sense of sin and coming wrath, we are not to be called cruel, or harsh, or too plain and outspoken, if we begin in the very same way—by convincing you of sin, and showing every unconverted soul among you how utterly undone you are.

But I now come to the second work of the Spirit, from which he is properly called the Comforter: " He will convince the world of righteousness." When he has first *broken the bones* under a sense of sin, then he reveals the good Physician, and makes the very bones which he hath broken to rejoice. When he has first revealed the coming storm of wrath, so that the sinner knows not where to flee, then he opens the secret chamber, and whispers: Come in hither; it may be thou shalt be hid in the day of the Lord's anger. When he has cast light into the sinner's bosom, and let him see how every action of his life condemns him, and how vain it is to seek for any righteousness there, he then casts light upon the risen Saviour, and says: Look there. He shows the Saviour's finished sufferings and finished obedience, and says: All this is thine, if thou wilt believe on Jesus. Thus does the Spirit lead the soul to accept and close with Christ, freely offered in the Gospel. The first was the awakening work of the Spirit—this is the comforting work of the Spirit. And this shows you plainly that the second work of the faithful minister is to do the very same—to lead weary souls to Christ—to stand pointing not only to the coming deluge, but to the freely offered ark—pointing not only to the threatening storm, but to the strong tower of safety—directing the sinner's eye not only inwards to his sin, and misery, but outwards also, to the bleeding, dying, rising, reigning Saviour.

Brethren, he is no minister of Christ who only terrifies and awakens you—who only aims at the first work of the Spirit, to convince you of sin, and aims not at the second work of the Spirit, to convince you of righteousness. He would be like *a surgeon* who should tear off the bandages of your wounds, and lay open their deepest recesses, and then leave you like Israel with your sores not closed, neither bound up, neither mollified with ointment. He would be like a man who should awake you when your house was all on fire, and yet leave you without showing you any way of escape.

Brethren, let us rather be taught to follow in the footsteps of the blessed Spirit, the Comforter. He first convinces of sin, and then convinces of righteousness. And so brethren, bear with us, when we first awaken you to a sense of the dreadfulness of your sins, and then open the refuge and say: Come in hither—" hide thee as it were for a little moment, till the indignation be overpast."

I know there may be many of you quite offended because we preach Christ to the vilest of sinners. It was so with the Pharisees; and doubtless there are many Pharisees among us. When we enter into the haunts of wickedness and profligacy, and, in accents of tenderness, proclaim the simple message of redeeming love—that the wrath of God is abiding on sinners, but that Christ is a Saviour freely offered to them, just as they are; or when a child of sin and misery comes before us, and the minister of Christ first plainly tells of God's wrath against his sin, and then as plainly, and with all affection, of Christ's compassion, and freely offered righteousness— oh! how often the decent moral men of the world are affronted. The very imagination that the same Saviour is offered as freely to the veriest offscourings of vice as to themselves—this is more than they can bear. What! they cry; do you offer these wretches a Saviour before they have reformed their lives—before they have changed their character? I answer, Yes. The whole need not a physician, but they that are sick: and I beseech you to mark that this is the very way of the Spirit of God.

He is the Holy Spirit—of purer eyes than to behold iniquity. He is the Sanctifier of all that are in Jesus; and yet, when he has convinced a sinner of sin, his next work is to speak peace—to convince that sinner of righteousness. If you ask me, then, why I do not say to the child of sin and shame, Go and reform yourself— become honest and pure, and then I will invite you to the Saviour? I answer, Because even the Spirit, the Holy Spirit, the Sanctifier, does not do this. He first leads the soul into the wilderness, and then he allures it to come to Christ. He first shuts up the soul in prison under a sense of guilt, and then opens a door—reveals Christ an open refuge for the chief of sinners.

Brethren! do not forget it—he is the Comforter before he is the Sanctifier. Ah, then, do not blame us, if, as messengers of Christ, we tread in the very footsteps of that blessed Spirit. If even he, the holy sanctifying Spirit, whose very breath is all purity—if even he invites the vilest sinner to put on these beautiful garments—the divine righteousness of Jesus—do not say that we are favouring sin—that we are the enemies of morality, if we carry this message to the vilest of sinners: " Believe on the Lord Jesus, and thou shalt be saved."

I. *What is this righteousness ?*

I answer, It is the righteousness of Christ, wrought out in behalf of sinners. Now righteousness means righteousness with respect to the law. When a person has never broken the law, but has rendered complete obedience to it, that person is righteous. Righteousness consists of two parts—*first*, freedom from guilt; and *second*, worthiness in the sight of God.

1. *In the case of an unfallen angel*, for example, he may be called righteous in two ways. (1) He is negatively righteous, because he has never broken the law of God—he has never loved anything which God would not have him love—never done anything which God would not have him do—he has acquired no stain of guilt upon his snow-white garments. But, (2) He is positively righteous, because he has fulfilled the law of God. He has obeyed in all things his all-holy will. He has spread his ready wings on every errand which the Father commanded—ministering night and day to the heirs of salvation. In all things he has made it his meat and drink to do the will of his heavenly Father. So, then, he has not only kept his snowy garments clean, but he has gained the laurel wreath of obedience—he is worthy in the sight of God—God smiles on him as he approaches. Now, brethren, both of these put together make up a righteousness in the sight of God.

2. *In the case of unfallen Adam.* (1) He was negatively righteous. He was made free from all guilt. Innocent and pure he came from

100

the hands of his Maker. Not more truly did the calm rivers of Paradise reflect the blue heaven from their untroubled bosom, than did the tranquil bosom of unfallen Adam reflect the blessed image of God. His soul was spotless as the white robes of angels. His thoughts were all directed heavenward. He had not once broken the law of God, in thought, word, or deed. His will was even with God's will. He had no conscience of sin. But, (2) Adam did not acquire a positive righteousness; that is, the righteousness of one who has obeyed the law—who has done the will of God. He was put into Paradise in order to acquire that righteousness. He was put there in pure and holy garments, to acquire the laurel wreath of obedience—like the holy angels. But man fell without acquiring this meritorious righteousness in the sight of God. Now, brethren, both these put together—both freedom from guilt and perfect obedience—make up a perfect righteousness in the sight of God.

3. I come, then, to show that the righteousness of Christ, freely offered to sinners, includes both of these. *There is freedom from guilt in Christ,* because he is gone to the Father. When he came to this world, he was not free from guilt. He had no sin of his own. Even in his mother's womb he was called " That holy thing;" but yet he did not breathe one moment in this world, but under the load of guilt. When he was an infant in the manger, he was under guilt; when he was a man of sorrows and acquainted with grief, he was under guilt; when he sat down wearied at the well, he was under guilt; when he was in that dreadful agony in the garden, when his sweat was as it were great drops of blood, he was under guilt; when he was in his last agony on the cross, he was under guilt. He had no sin of his own, and yet these are his words: " Innumerable evils have compassed me about: mine iniquities have taken hold upon me, so that I am not able to look up; they are more than the hairs of mine head; therefore my heart faileth me."

Inquiry. How do you know that Christ was under guilt ?

Answer. (1) Because he was under pain. He suffered the pains of infancy in the manger—he suffered weariness, and hunger, and thirst, and great agonies in the garden and on the cross. But God has eternally connected guilt and pain. If there were no guilt, there could be no pain. (2) Because God hid his face from him: "My God, my God." Now, God hides his face from nothing but guilt; therefore Christ was bearing the sins of many. He was all over with guilt. He was as guilty in the sight of God as if he had committed all the sins of his people. What wonder, then, that God hid his face even from his own Son?

But Christ is now free from guilt. He is risen and gone to the Father. When a man is lying under a debt—if he pays it, then he is free from the debt. So Christ was lying under our sins, but he suffered all the punishment, and now is free; he rose, and we see him no more. When a man is banished for so many years, it is unlawful for him to return to his country till the time has expired, and the punishment is borne; but when the time is expired, then he is free from guilt in the eye of the law. He may come back to his home and his country once more. So Christ was banished from the bosom of the Father for a time. God hid his face from him; but when he had borne all that God saw fit to lay on him, then he was free from guilt—he was free to return; and so he did—he rose, and went back to the bosom of the Father, from which he came. Do you not see, then, trembling sinner, that there is freedom from all guilt in Christ? He is quite free—he never shall suffer any more. He is now without sin, and when he comes again, he is coming without sin. If you will become one with him, you, too, are free from guilt—you are as free as Christ is—you are as safe from being punished as if you were in heaven with Christ. If you believe on Christ, you are one with him—a member of his body; and as sure as Christ your Head is now passed from the darkness of God's anger into the light of his countenance, so surely are you, O believer, passed from darkness into God's marvellous light. O what a blessed word was that of Christ, just before he ascended: "I go to my Father and your Father, to my God and your God!" God is now as much ours as he is Christ's.

Inquiry. What good is it to me that Christ is free from guilt?

Answer. Christ is offered to you as your Saviour. *There is perfect obedience in Christ,* because he hath gone to the Father, and we see him no more. When he came to this world, he came not only to suffer, but to do—not only to be a dying Saviour, but also a doing Saviour—not only to suffer the curse which the first Adam had brought upon the world, but to render the obedience which the first Adam had left undone. From the cradle to the cross he obeyed the will of God from the heart. When he came into the world, his word was: " Lo ! I come; in the volume of the book it is written of me, I delight to do thy will, O God; yea, thy law is within my heart." When he was in the midst of his obedience, still he did not change his mind. He says: " I have meat to eat that ye know not of: my meat is to do the will of him that sent me, and to finish his work." And when he was going out of the world, still his word was: " I have finished the work which thou gavest me to do." So that it is true what an apostle says—that he was " obedient even unto death." The whole law is summed up in these two commands—That we love God and our neighbour. Christ did both. (1) He loved God perfectly, as God says in the 91st Psalm: " Because he hath set his love upon me, therefore will I deliver him; I will set him on high." (2) He loved his neighbour as himself. It was out of love to men that he came into the world at all; and everything he did and everything he suffered in the world, was out of love to his neighbour. It was out of love to men that he performed the greatest part of his obedience, namely, the laying down his life. This was the principal errand upon which he came into the world. This was the most dreadful and difficult command which God laid upon him; and yet he obeyed. But a short while before he was betrayed, God gave him an awful view of his coming wrath, in the garden of Gethsemane. He set down the cup before him, and showed that it was a cup without any mixture of mercy in it; and yet Christ obeyed: his human nature shrunk back from it, and he prayed: " If it be possible, let this cup pass from me;" but he did not waver one moment from complete obedience, for he adds: " Nevertheless, not as I will, but as thou wilt."

Now this is the obedience of Christ, and we know that it is perfect. (1) Because he was the Son of God, and all that he did must be perfect. (2) Because he has gone to the Father. He is ascended into the presence of God. And how did the Father

103

receive him ? We are told in the 110th Psalm. A door is opened in heaven, and we are suffered to hear the very words with which God receives his Son: " The Lord said unto my Lord, Sit thou on my right hand, till I make thine enemies thy footstool."

So, then, God did not send him back, as one who had not obeyed perfectly enough. God did not forbid him his presence, as one unworthy to be accepted; but God highly exalted him—looked upon him as worthy of much honour—worthy of a seat on the throne at his right hand. Oh ! how plain that Christ is accepted with the Father !—how plain that his righteousness is most lovely and all divine in the sight of God the Father !

Hearken, then, trembling sinner !—this righteousness is offered to you. It was wrought just for sinners like you, and for none else; it is for no other use but just to cover naked sinners. This is the clothing of wrought gold, and the raiment of needlework. This is the wedding-garment—the fine linen, white and clean. Oh ! put ye on the Lord Jesus. Why should ye refuse your own mercies ? Become one with Christ, by believing, and you are not only pardoned, as I showed before, but you are righteous in the sight of God; not only shall you never be cast into hell, but you shall surely be carried into heaven—as surely as Christ is now there. Become one with Christ, and even this moment you are lovely in the sight of God— comely, through his comeliness put upon you. You are as much accepted in the sight of God as is the Son of Man, the Beloved, that sits on his right hand. The Spirit shall be given you, as surely as he is given to Christ. He is given to Christ as the oil of gladness, wherewith he is anointed above his fellows. You are as sure to wear a crown of glory, as that Christ is now wearing his. You are as sure to sit upon Christ's throne, as that Christ is now sitting on his Father's throne. O weep for joy, happy believer ! O sing for gladness of heart: " For I am persuaded that neither death, nor life, nor angels, nor principalities, nor powers, nor things present, nor things to come, nor height, nor depth, nor any other creature, shall be able to separate us from the love of God, which is in Christ Jesus our Lord."

104

II. *What is conviction of righteousness ?*

Let us show what it is not.

1. *It is not any impression on the imagination.* Just as men have often imaginary terrors, so men have also imaginary views of Christ, and of the glory of being in Christ. Sometimes they think they see Christ with the bodily eye; or sometimes they think they hear words,borne in upon their mind, telling of the beauty of Christ. Now this is not conviction of righteousness. Indeed, such things may accompany true conversion. There is no impossibility in it. Stephen and Paul both saw Christ, and most of you remember a very singular example of something similar in more modern times.[1] But, however this may be, one thing is certain, that conviction of righteousness is very different from this. It is a far higher and nobler thing—given only by the Spirit of God. Blessed are they who have not seen, and yet have believed.

2. *It is not a revelation of any new truths not contained in the Bible.* When the Spirit revealed Christ to the apostles and prophets of old, he revealed new truths concerning Christ. But when he convinces a sinner of the righteousness of Christ, he does it by opening up the truths contained in the Bible. If he revealed new truths, then we might put away the Bible, and sit alone, waiting for the Spirit to come down on us. But this is contrary to the Bible and experience. David prays: " Open thou mine eyes, that I may see wonders." Where ? Not in heaven above nor earth beneath, but, " out of thy law." It is through the truth that the Spirit always works in our hearts: " Sanctify them through thy truth; thy Word is truth." Therefore, when you look for conviction of righteousness, you are not to look for new truths not in the Bible, but for divine light cast upon old truths already in the Bible.

3. *It is not mere head knowledge of what the Bible says of Christ and his righteousness.* Most unconverted men read their Bibles, and many of them understand very wonderfully the doctrine of imputed righteousness; yet these have no conviction of righteousness. All awakened souls read their Bibles very anxiously, with much prayer and weeping; and many of them seem to understand very clearly

[1] Alluding to a recent occurrence.

the truth that Christ is an all-sufficient righteousness; yet they tell us they cannot close with Christ—they cannot apply him to their own case. Again: the devils believe and tremble. The devil has plainly much knowledge of the Bible; and from the quotations he made to Christ, it is plain that he understood much of the work of redemption; and yet he is none the better for it—he only trembles and gnashes his teeth the more. Ah, my friends ! if you have no more than head knowledge of Christ and his righteousness, you have no more than devils have—you have never been convinced of righteousness.

What is it ?

Answer. It is a sense of the preciousness and fitness of Christ, as he is revealed in the Gospel.

1. I have said it is a sense of the preciousness of Christ, that you may see plainly that it is no imaginary feeling of Christ's beauty; that it is no seeing of Christ with the bodily eyes; that it is no mere knowledge of Christ and of his righteousness in the head—but a feeling of his preciousness in the heart. I before showed you that there is all the difference in the world between knowing a thing and feeling a thing—between having a knowledge of a thing, and having a sense of it. There is all the difference in the world between knowing that honey is sweet, and tasting that it is sweet, so as to have a sense of its sweetness. There is a great difference between knowing that a person is beautiful, and actually seeing, so as to have a present sense of the beauty of the person. There is a great difference between knowing that a glove will fit the hand, and putting it on, so as to have a sense of its fitness. Just so, brethren, there is all the difference in the world between having a head knowledge of Christ and of his righteousness, and having a heart feeling of his fitness and preciousness. The first may be acquired from flesh and blood, or from books; the second must come from the Spirit of God.

2. Again, it is a sense of the fitness of Christ. It is conceivable that a person may have a sense of Christ's preciousness, without having a sense of his fitness. Some awakened souls appear to feel that Christ is very precious; and yet they dare not put on Christ:

106

they seem to want a sense of his fitness to their case. They cry out: " O how precious a Saviour he is to all his people ! "—" O that I were one of his people ! O that I were hidden in his bleeding side ! " And yet they have no sense of his fitness to be their Saviour; they do not cry out: " He just fits my case !—he is the very Saviour for me ! " For, if they felt this, they would be at peace—their lips would overflow with joy. But no; they dare not appropriate Christ. Now, then, conviction of righteousness is to have such a sense of Christ as leads us, without hesitation, to put on Christ; and that I have called a sense of his fitness.

It gives me no comfort to know that Christ is a precious Saviour to others, unless I know that he is a precious Saviour to me. If the deluge is coming on—the windows of heaven opening, and the fountains of the great deep broken up—it gives me no peace to know that there is an ark for others, unless you tell me that it is an ark for me. You may tell me of Christ's righteousness for ever, and of the safety of all that are in him; but if you would comfort me by the news, you must convince me that that righteousness answers me, and is offered to me. Now, this is what the Spirit does when he convinces of righteousness. This, and this only, is conviction of righteousness.

O brethren ! it is no slight work of nature to persuade a soul, even an anxious soul, to put on Christ. If it were a natural work, then natural means might do it; but it is a supernatural work, and the hand of the Spirit must do it. Flesh and blood cannot reveal Christ unto you, but my Father which is in heaven. No man can call Jesus Lord, but by the Holy Ghost.

Let me speak a word to three classes.

1. *To the unawakened*. See how far you are from salvation. Many of you may be saying just now in your heart: " It is quite true I am not at present a saved person; but I am not very far from the kingdom of God. I have just to repent and believe on Jesus, and then I am saved. And since this is so short and simple a matter, I may do it any time. I may enjoy the world and its pleasures a little longer; and then, when death or disease threatens me, it may be good time to become anxious." Now, all this argument proceeds

107

upon a falsehood. You think you are not far off from salvation; but, ah! my friend, you are as far from salvation as any one can be that is in the land of the living. There is only one case in which you could be farther from salvation, and that is in hell. You are as far from salvation as any one that is out of hell. (1) In my last discourse, I showed you that there must be a divine work upon your heart before you can repent. You may have much head knowledge of sin without the Spirit, but he only can convince you of sin. That Spirit is a sovereign Spirit. He is given to the children of God as often as they ask him; but he is not at the bidding of unconverted men. You cannot bid him come when you fall sick, or when you are going to die; or if you should bid him, he has nowhere promised to obey. (2) And now, I wish you to see that there is a second divine work needful on your heart before you can believe. The Spirit must convince you of Christ's righteousness. Flesh and blood cannot reveal Christ unto you, but my Father which is in heaven. God is a sovereign God. He hath mercy upon whom he will have mercy. He is not at the bidding of unconverted men. He has nowhere promised to bring to Christ all whom he awakens. Oh! how plain that you are as far from salvation as any soul can be that is out of hell. And can you be easy when you are at such a distance from salvation? Can you go now, and sit down to a game of chance—to while away the time between this and judgment? Can you go and laugh and be merry in your sins? How truly, then, did Solomon say: "The laughter of fools is like the crackling of thorns under a pot"—a loud noise for a moment, then everlasting silence—a short blaze, and a dark eternity.

2. *To the awakened.*

(1) Remember, unless you attain to conviction of righteousness, your conviction of sin will be all in vain. Remember, anxiety for the soul does not save the soul. Sailors in a shipwreck are very anxious. They cry much to God in prayers and tears; and yet, though they are anxious men, they are not saved men—the vessel goes to pieces, and all are drowned. Travellers in a wilderness may be very anxious—their hearts may die within them; yet that does not show that they are safe—they may perish in the burning sands.

So you are much afraid of the wrath of God, and it may be God has, in mercy, stirred up these anxieties in your bosom: but you are not yet saved—unless you come to Christ all will be in vain. Many are convinced who are never converted. Many are now in hell who were once as anxious to escape as you.

(2) Remember, God only can give you this conviction. The Spirit convinces of righteousness. It is not flesh and blood that can give you a sense of the preciousness of Christ. It is true, the Bible and preaching are the means through which God works this conviction. He always works through the truth—never without the truth. If you be truly awakened, I know how anxiously you will wait on these means—how you will search the Scriptures with tears, and lose no opportunity of hearing the preached Word. But still, the Bible and preaching are only means of themselves—they can only make natural impressions on your mind. God only can make supernatural impressions. Cry, then, to God.

(3) But remember, God is a sovereign God. Do not cry to him to convert you, as if it were a debt he owed you. There is only one thing you can claim from God as a right, and that is a place in hell. If you think you have any claim on God, you are deceiving yourself. You are not yet convinced of sin. Lie at the feet of God as a sovereign God—a God who owes you nothing but punishment. Lie at his feet as the God who alone can reveal Christ unto you. Cry night and day that he would reveal Christ unto you—that he would shine into your darkness, and give you the light of the knowledge of the glory of God in the face of Christ. One glimpse of that face will give you peace. It may be you shall be hid in the day of the Lord's anger.

3. *To those of you who have come to Christ.* Oh, what miracles of grace you are ! Twice over you are saved by grace. When you were loathsome in your sins, and yet asleep, the Spirit awakened you. Thousands were sleeping beside you. He left thousands to perish, but awakened you.

Again: though awakened, you were as loathsome as ever: you were as vile in the sight of God as ever, only you dreaded hell. In some respects you were more wicked than the unawakened world

109

around you. They would not come to Christ, because they felt no need. But you felt your need, yet would not come. You made God a liar more than they, yet God had mercy on you. He led you to Christ—convinced you of righteousness. So you are twice over saved by grace. " O to grace how great a debtor ! " " What shall I render to the Lord for all his benefits ? " Will you not love him with all your heart ? Will you not serve him with all you have ? And when he says: Feed this poor orphan for my sake, will you not say: Lord, when I give for thee, it is more blessed to give than to receive ?

Dundee, Feb. 11, 1837.

CHRIST PRESENT, YET UNKNOWN

" Have I been so long time with you, and yet hast thou not known me, Philip ? "—JOHN xiv. 9.

CHRIST had been with his disciples night and day during the three years of his ministry. They had seen him in all situations—walking on the sea—feeding the multitudes—raising the dead. They had heard all his words in the synagogues—in the temple—in the fields. He had fed them with milk, and not with strong meat— giving them instruction just as they were able to bear it; and yet it is amazing how blind they were to his glory and greatness. They were foolish, and slow of heart to believe all that the prophets had spoken concerning him, and all that he had spoken concerning himself.

This was the last night that Jesus was to be with his disciples, and his heart was full of a tenderness which is not of the world. But the more full and tender his holy heart became, the more dull and stupid did his disciples become. " Philip saith unto him,

110

Lord, show us the Father, and it sufficeth us. Jesus saith unto him, Have I been so long time with you, and yet hast thou not known me, Philip ? "

Two things give this reply a peculiar tenderness: 1. He reminds Philip that he had been with him. He was equal with the Father—was in the bosom of God, and yet had come and dwelt with them. He had left the company of the worshipping angels to company with them—the King of glory dwelt with worms ! Had he smiled on them from heaven, that would have been wonderful; but he says: " I have been with you—with you by the way-side and by the well—with you on the sea and in the wilderness—I have been your elder brother—and yet have you not known me ? " 2. That he had been long with them: " So long time." Had it been for a moment that the Son of God had visited the earth, O it would have been wonderful ! but it was for years. Three years he had gone in and out with them. He had taught them—opened the Scriptures—taught them to pray—led them like an elder brother all that time, willing to explain everything to them. O, then, what tenderness there is in this word: " Have I been *so* long ? "

Doctrine. When Christ has been long with any soul, he expects that soul to know him.

I. *Let us speak of Christians.*

1. *Christ has been with believers.* He says to every child of God: " I have been with you." (1) In conversion. It is the revealing of Christ to the soul which brings it to peace. When Christ revealed himself to Saul, then he fell to the ground, and cried: " Lord, what wilt thou have me to do ? " So it is still. Christ is with the soul in conversion. Are you converted ? Then you have been with Jesus, and Jesus has been with you. (2) In the wilderness Christ is with the soul. The soul leans on the Beloved coming up out of the wilderness. If you be believers at all, you know what it is to have the sweet strengthening presence of the Beloved. (3) In affliction. Christ is peculiarly near in the fire and in the water: " When thou passest through the waters I will be with thee." And again: " I will not leave you orphans; I will come to you." If you be Christians,

111

you have felt that Christ is with you in the day of adversity. When doors are shut, Jesus stands in the midst, and says: "Peace." (4) In prayer: "Where two or three are gathered together in my name, there am I in the midst of them." He is near at our breathing—at our cry—to offer up our prayer with much incense. He never misses the simplest cry of the simplest believer. Christians, you know that Christ is with you in prayer. It is this which gives you boldness at the throne of grace.

2. *Christ has been long time with believers:* "Have I been so long time with you?" he says. Christ had been only three years with the disciples when he said this. He has been a much longer time with some of you. Look back, dear Christians, on the way by which he has led you. This day is an eminence—stand upon it, and look back. How long time has Christ been with you? Some of you who are up in years were converted in youth—you have had a life-time with Christ. He has been with you as your surety—as your strength—as your elder brother—as your advocate with his Father. He has been with you thus for many, many years. If some great nobleman were to come and pay you a visit, and be an intimate friend with you, you would think it a great thing. But O how much greater is this! Christ has been with you—Christ knows your name—Christ has often said of you, as of Zaccheus: "To-day I must abide at thy house."

Some of you may have been but lately brought to the knowledge of Christ. You have but lately opened the door and let him in. Still he has been long with you. To have Christ with you for a single day is to have him long with you—it is so great an honour—it is so rich a blessing. O there is a day at hand when you will reckon a moment spent with Christ as more than all your life besides! "A day spent in thy courts is better than a thousand."

3. *Christ reproves believers for knowing so little of him:* "Hast thou not known me, Philip?" The apostles knew much of Christ, and yet they were slow of heart to believe *all*. So is it with Christians now. They know much of Christ, yet they are slow of heart to believe all. There are many signs that Christians do not know Christ.

112

1. *Little happiness among Christians.* There is very little sense of being pardoned. Some of you, who appear to be Christians, would almost start were I to ask you if you feel the forgiveness of sins. You seem to fear it, as an unlawful question—as if it were a secret not for you to know. Is this the case with you ? Ah ! how truly Christ may say: " Have I been so long time with you, yet hast thou not known me ? " Has not Christ been revealed to you a crucified Saviour—the wrath of God all poured out on him ? " O fools, and slow of heart to believe all that the prophets have spoken ! "

2. *Little communion with God.* When you stand in the sunshine, you feel the warm beams of the sun; so, when you stand in Christ, you should feel the warm beams of his love. There is little of this. Believers are said to be " a people near to God." Entering through the rent veil, they draw near to the Father—they dwell in his secret place, and abide under his shadow. There is little, very little of this. How truly may Christ say: " Have I been so long time with you, and yet hast thou not known me ? "

3. *Little holiness.* If Christians had an eye on a reigning, praying, coming Saviour, O how different persons they would be ! What manner of persons ought ye to be in all holy conversation and godliness, seeing ye look for such things ? (1) How much covetousness there is among some of you that seem to be Christians—how much calling your money your own—hugging it all to yourself—to please yourself—to be enjoyed by yourself; and all this when the cause of Christ calls loud for sacrifices ! (2) How much bitterness there is among some of you that seem to be Christians—how much of a proud, unforgiving spirit—keeping up the remembrance of injuries—nursing your wrath ! (3) How much likeness to the world in your feasts and luxuries—in your trifling, yea, sinful amusements; and, above all, in your conversation ! Who that hears you speak, would know that ever you had been with Jesus, or he with you ? Why is all this ? *Ans.* Because you know so little of Christ. For all that Christ has been so long with you, yet you know almost nothing of him. Ah ! do not let this year go without resolving to know more of Christ. He is with you still. A little while, and ye shall not see him. A few days, and you may see no more of him.

113

Your days of grace may be nearly ended. Many of you will not see the close of another year. Walk in the light, while ye have the light. Know Christ, and then ye shall be like him.

II. *Let us speak of the awakened.*

1. *Christ is with awakened souls.* (1) He awakened them. No man is naturally anxious about his soul. It is a work of Christ on the soul. When the lightning has passed through a wood, as you look upon one tree and another that has been split by its mighty flash, you say : Ah! the lightning has been here. So, when you see a heart split and broken under a sense of its lost condition, you may say: Christ has been here. Are any of you awakened ? Christ has been with you. He saw you in your sin and folly. He pitied you— he drew near—he touched your heart, and made you feel yourself lost, in order that you might seek him as a Saviour. Do not doubt Christ has been with you. (2) He is seeking awakened souls, and therefore is with them. When a shepherd goes into the mountains in search of lost sheep, he seeks peculiarly those which are bleeding and torn, making the valleys resound with their sad bleatings; he bends over the wounded sheep. When a good physician enters the hospital, he hurries to the beds of the most diseased—of those who are piteously groaning under their pains; he bends over such. So does Christ seek bleeding, groaning souls, with a peculiar care. His word is: " He hath sent me to bind up the broken-hearted; he hath given me the tongue of the learned to speak a word in season to them that are weary. Are you an awakened soul ? Then you may be quite sure Christ is with you—bending over you.

2. *He is often with them a long time.* Some persons continue under convictions of sin for a long time; some for months and years. This year, I doubt not, has seen many souls awakened. Now Christ waits long upon these souls. He stands at the door all the day: " I have stretched out my hands all the day to a gainsaying and disobedient people;" and then, when night comes, as he still stands and waits: " My head is filled with dew, and my locks with the drops of the night." Are there any awakened souls hearing me ? Christ

114

has been long with you. The Bible has been his witness; it has been with you night and day. His ministers have told you of Jesus; they have waited and been long-suffering with you. Christ himself has bended over you. Never did a beggar stand at the door of a rich man so long as Christ has stood at your door.

3. *Still many have not known him.* Although Christ be so long with awakened souls, yet many will not know him. It is life eternal to know him. It would heal all their pains if they would only look upon him; but they will not look. Some of you are in this state. It is your sin, and it is your misery. Christ has long stood at your door and knocked. If you had opened, you would have seen a bleeding Saviour—a surety—a righteousness. You would have looked to him, and been lightened; but you would not open. Christ has stood and cried: " If any man thirst, let him come to me and drink." You feel very thirsty, yet you do not come to Christ to drink. Christ has cried: " Come unto me, all ye that labour and are heavy laden, and I will give you rest." You are bent down with your burden, yet you will not come to Christ in order to have life. Christ has cried: " Follow me; he that followeth me shall not walk in darkness." You vibrate between him and the world. You cling to the world, even though you are miserable. How long shall it be thus ? Have I been so long time with you, and yet hast thou not known me, poor anxious soul ? Remember, some have lived anxious, and died anxious. Remember, it will only increase your hell, that Christ was so long with you, and you would not know him. Turn to Christ now. Let not another year begin without knowing Jesus.

III. *Let us speak of the unawakened.*

1. *Christ is with them.* In one sense, he is not with them. They are without Christ, and without God in the world. In another sense, he is with them: " I know thy works." (1) He is with them in the house of God. It is wonderful to me how Christ persuades so many Christless people to come to the house of God; I never could explain it. Crowds followed Jesus; crowds follow him still. *Ques.* What brings you to the house of God ? It is the constraining grace of Christ. Here Christ is with you. Christ unlocks his treasure, and

says: "Come, buy, without money and without price." (2) He is with them in providences. O it is wonderful to see the providences of unawakened souls! Every one of them is from the hand of Christ: "I stand at the door and knock." In the year now past, Christ has striven with you in his providence. To some of you he hath come once and again. (3) He is with them in their sins. Christ is present at all their unholy feasts—hears all their unholy jests—is cognizant of all their desires—knows all their engagements: "I know thy works." Do you ever think when you are engaged in some silly game, that Christ is by your side? He sees the smile of satisfaction on your cheek, but he sees also the deluge of wrath that is over your soul. He sees you sporting yourself with your own deceivings—sitting on the brink of hell, yet "pleased with a rattle, tickled with a straw." What does he say? He says: "How long, ye simple ones, will ye love your simplicity?" and again: "Lord, let it alone this year also."

2. *He is with them a long time.* There is reason to think that Jesus strives with the soul from its earliest years—that he strives on to the last. Some good men have thought that Christ doth sometimes give over striving, and leaves the soul to be joined to its idols; but perhaps it is more accordant with Scripture to say that Jesus waits all the day. How long a time Christ has pleaded with some of you! This day, another year of striving with you is finished. Think on this. O the long-suffering of Christ!

3. *Yet they do not know him.* Ah! there is reason to think that many of you are as ignorant of Christ as the day I began my ministry among you; yea, as ignorant as the day you were born. If you knew Christ, it would break your heart with a sense of sin; but your heart is whole within you. If you knew Christ, it would drive you to seek an interest in him; but you seek him not. Hark how tenderly the Saviour pleads with you this day: "Have I been so long time with you?" O it will be one of the greatest miseries of hell, to remember how often Christ was with you in this house of prayer—in your providences—ay, in your sins; and you would not look at him! to remember how often he was set forth a broken Saviour in the sacrament—preached by his servants a free Saviour—how often he

116

bended over you, and wept over you, and ye would have none of him !

O sirs ! I fear this year will witness against you in the judgment-day ! I fear there are many of you who will accuse me in that day, and say: Why did you not speak plainer—louder—oftener ? Why did you not knock oftener at our doors, to tell us and our children of Christ, the way to glory ?—was it not worth more effort to save us from an eternal hell ? Ah ! dear friends, be wise. Many of you will not see another year come to a close. If there be fifty—O how dreadful !—you may be among that fifty; nay, if there be forty, thirty, twenty, ten, still you may be among the ten. If there be but one, you may be that one. O it will be an awful word in that day: " I was a long time with you, but you would not know me ! "

Dundee, Dec. 31, 1837.

WHO SHALL SEPARATE US ?

" Who shall separate us from the love of Christ ? Shall tribulation, or distress, or persecution, or famine, or nakedness, or peril, or sword ? As it is written, For thy sake we are killed all the day long; we are accounted as sheep for the slaughter. Nay, in all these things we are more than conquerors through him that loved us."—Rom. viii. 35–37.

IN this passage there are three very remarkable questions:

1. " Who shall lay anything to the charge of God's elect ? " Paul stands forth like a herald, and he looks up to the holy angels, and down to the accusing devils, and round about on a scowling world, and into conscience, and he asks, Who can accuse one whom God has chosen, and Christ has washed ? It is God who justifieth. The holy God has declared believers clean every whit.

117

2. "Who shall condemn?" Paul looks round all the judges of the world—all who are skilled in law and equity; he looks upward to the holy angels, whose superhuman sight pierces deep and far into the righteous government of God; he looks up to God, the judge of all, who must do right—whose ways are equal and perfect righteousness—and he asks, Who shall condemn? It is Christ that died. Christ has paid the uttermost farthing: so that every judge must cry out, There is now no condemnation.

3. "Who shall separate us from the love of Christ?" Again, he looks round all created worlds—he looks at the might of the mightiest archangel—the satanic power of legions of devils—the rage of a God-defying world—the united forces of all created things; and, when he sees sinners folded in the arms of Jesus, he cries, "Who shall separate us from the love of Christ?" Not all the forces of ten thousand worlds combined, for Jesus is greater than all. "We are more than conquerors through him that loved us."

The love of Christ! Paul says: "The love of Christ passeth knowledge." It is like the blue sky, into which you may see clearly, but the real vastness of which you cannot measure. It is like the deep, deep sea, into whose bosom you can look a little way, but its depths are unfathomable. It has a breadth without a bound, length without end, height without top, and depth without bottom. If holy Paul said this, who was so deeply taught in divine things—who had been in the third heaven, and seen the glorified face of Jesus—how much more may we, poor and weak believers, look into that love and say: It passeth knowledge!

There are three things in these words, of which I would speak. 1. The love of Christ. 2. The question, Who would separate us from it? 3. The truth, that whoever or whatever they are, they shall not be able.

I. *I would speak of the love of Christ.*

1. *When did it begin?*—In the past eternity: "Then I was by him as one brought up with him: and I was daily his delight, rejoicing always before him; rejoicing in the habitable part of the earth; and my delights were with the sons of men." (Prov. viii. 30, 31.) This

118

river of love began to flow before the world was—from everlasting, from the beginning, or ever the earth was. Christ's love to us is as old as the Father's love to the Son. This river of light began to stream from Jesus toward us before the beams poured from the sun—before the rivers flowed to the ocean—before angel loved angel, or man loved man. Before creatures were, Christ loved us. This is a great deep—who can fathom it ? This love passeth knowledge.

2. *Who was it that loved ?* It was Jesus, the Son of God, the second person of the blessed Godhead. His name is, " Wonderful, Counsellor, The Mighty God, The Everlasting Father, The Prince of Peace," " King of kings and Lord of lords," Immanuel, Jesus the Saviour, the only begotten of his Father. His beauty is perfect: he is the brightness of his Father's glory, and the express image of his person. All the purity, majesty, and love of Jehovah dwell fully in him. He is the bright and morning Star: he is the Sun of righteousness and the Light of the world: he is the Rose of Sharon and the Lily of the valleys—fairer than the children of men. His riches are infinite: he could say, " All that the Father hath is mine." He is Lord of all. All the crowns in heaven were cast at his feet—all angels and seraphs were his servants—all worlds his domain. His doings were infinitely glorious. By him were all things created that are in heaven and that are in earth, visible and invisible. He called the things that are not as though they were—worlds started into being at his word. *Yet he loved us.* It is much to be loved by one greater in rank than ourselves—to be loved by an angel; but, O, to be loved by the Son of God !—this is wonderful—it passeth knowledge.

3. *Whom did he love ?* He loved us ! He came into the world " to save sinners, of whom I am the chief." Had he loved one as glorious as himself, we would not have wondered. Had he loved the holy angels, that reflected his pure, bright image, we would not have wondered. Had he loved the lovely among the sons of men—the amiable, the gentle, the kind, the rich, the great, the noble—it would not have been so great a wonder. But, ah ! he loved sinners—the vilest sinners—the poorest, meanest, guiltiest wretches that crawl upon the ground. Manasseh, who murdered his own children,

was one whom he loved; Zaccheus, the grey-haired swindler, was another; blaspheming Paul was a third; the wanton of Samaria was another; the dying thief was another; and the lascivious Corinthians were more. " And such were some of you." We were black as hell when he looked on us—we were hell-worthy, under his Father's wrath and curse—and yet he loved us, and said: I will die for them. " Thou hast loved me out of the pit of corruption," each saved one can say. Oh, brethren! this is strange love: he that was so great, and lovely, and pure, chose us, who were mean and filthy with sin, that he might wash and purify, and present us to himself. This love passeth knowledge!

4. *What did this love cost him?* When Jacob loved Rachel, he served seven years for her—he bore the summer's heat and winter's cold. But Jesus bore the hot wrath of God, and the winter blast of his Father's anger, for those he loved. Jonathan loved David with more than the love of women, and for his sake he bore the cruel anger of his father, Saul. But Jesus, out of love to us, bore the wrath of his Father poured out without mixture. It was the love of Christ that made him leave the love of his Father, the adoration of angels, and the throne of glory. It was love that made him not despise the Virgin's womb—it was love that brought him to the manger at Bethlehem—it was love that drove him into the wilderness; love made him a man of sorrows—love made him hungry, and thirsty, and weary—love made him hasten to Jerusalem—love led him to gloomy, dark Gethsemane—love bound and dragged him to the judgment hall—love nailed him to the cross—love bowed his head beneath the amazing load of his Father's anger. " Greater love hath no man than this." " I am the good Shepherd; the good Shepherd giveth his life for the sheep."

Sinners were sinking beneath the red-hot flames of hell; he plunged in and swam through the awful surge, and gathered his own into his bosom. The sword of justice was bare and glittering, ready to destroy us; He, the man that was God's fellow, opened his bosom and let the stroke fall on him. We were set up as a mark for God's arrows of vengeance; Jesus came between, and they pierced him through and through—every arrow that should have pierced our souls stuck fast in him. He, his own self, bare our sins in his own body on the tree. As far as east is from the west, so far hath he removed our transgressions from us. This is the love of Christ that passeth knowledge. This is what is set before you to-day in the broken bread and poured-out wine. This is what we shall see on the throne—a Lamb as it had been slain. This will be the matter of our song through eternity: " Worthy is the Lamb ! "

1. *O the joy of being in the love of Christ !* Are you in this amazing love ? Has he loved you out of the pit of corruption ? Then, he will wash you, and make you a king and a priest unto God. He will wash you in his own blood whiter than the snow—he will cleanse you from all your filthiness and from all your idols. A new heart also will he give you. He will keep your conscience clean, and your heart right with God. He will put his Holy Spirit within you, and make you pray with groanings that cannot be uttered. He will justify you—he will pray for you—he will glorify you. All the world may oppose you—dear friends may die and forsake you—you may be left alone in the wilderness; still you will not be alone— Christ will love you still.

2. *O the misery of being out of the love of Christ !* If Christ loves you not, how vain all other loves ! Your friends may love you— your neighbours may be kind to you—the world may praise you— ministers may love your souls; but, if Christ love you not, all creature-love will be vain. You will be unwashed, unpardoned, unholy—you will sink into hell, and all the creatures will stand around and be unable to reach out a hand to help you.

3. *How shall I know that I am in the love of Christ ?* By your being drawn to Christ: " I have loved thee with an everlasting love, therefore with loving-kindness have I drawn thee." Have you seen something attractive in Jesus ? The world are attracted by beauty, or dress, or glittering jewels—have you been attracted to Christ by his good ointments ? This is the mark of all who are graven on Christ's heart—they come to him; they see Jesus to be precious. The easy world see no preciousness in Christ; they prize a lust higher, the smile of the world higher, money higher, pleasure higher; but those whom Christ loves he draws after him by the sight of his

preciousness. Have you thus followed him, prized him—as a drowning sinner cleaved to him ?—then he will in no wise cast you out—in no wise, not for all you have done against him. " But I spent my best days in sin"—Still I will in no wise cast you out. " I lived in open sin "—I will in no wise cast you out. " But I have sinned against light and conviction "—Still I will in no wise cast you out. " But I am a backslider "—Still the arms of his love are open to enfold your poor guilty soul, and he will not cast you out.

II. *Many would separate us from Christ's love.*

From the beginning of the world it has been the great aim of Satan to separate believers from the love of Christ; and though he never has succeeded in the case of a single soul, yet still he tries it as eagerly as he did at first. The moment he sees the Saviour lift a lost sheep upon his shoulder, from that hour he plies all his efforts to pluck down the poor saved sheep from its place of rest. The moment the pierced hand of Jesus is laid on a poor, trembling, guilty sinner, from that hour does Satan try to pluck him out of Jesus' hand.

1. *He did this in old times:* " As it is written, For thy sake we are killed all the day long; we are accounted as sheep for the slaughter." (Verse 36.) This is a cry taken from the Book of Psalms. God's people in all ages have been hated and persecuted by Satan and the world. Observe, (1) The reason: " For thy sake "—because they were like Jesus, and belonged to Jesus. (2) The time: " All day long "—from morning till night. The world have a perpetual hatred against true believers, so that we have to say at evening: " Would God it were morning; and at morning, Would God it were evening." They have no other perpetual hatred. (3) The manner: " We are accounted as sheep for the slaughter." The world care no more for ill-treating a Christian than the butcher does when he lays hold of a sheep for the slaughter. The very drunkards make a song of us. Such was the cry of believers of old. The same cry has been heard amid the snowy heights of Piedmont; and, in later days, amid the green hills and valleys of Scotland. And we are miserably deceived if we flatter ourselves that the same cry will not be heard again. Is the devil changed ? Does he love Christ and his dear

people any better ? Is the worldly heart changed ? Does it hate God and God's people any less than it did ? Ah ! no. I have a deep conviction that, if God only withdraw his restraining grace, the flood-gates of persecution will soon break loose again; and many of you, left unconverted under our ministry, will turn out bloody persecutors—you will yet avenge yourselves for the sermons that have pricked your hearts.

2. *The apostle names seven forms in which trouble comes.* Two of them relate to the troubles that are common to man, and five to those that are more peculiar to the children of God.

(1) *Tribulation and distress:* " Man that is born of a woman is of few days, and full of trouble. He cometh forth as a flower, and is cut down; he fleeth also as a shadow, and continueth not." God's children are not freed from distresses—sickness, poverty, loss of friends. Jesus said to them: " In the world ye shall have tribulation." " Whom I love I rebuke and chasten." Now, Satan tries to take advantage of these times of tribulation, to separate the soul from the love of Christ; he tempts the believer to despise the chastening of the Lord—to plunge into business, or among worldly friends, or to follow worldly means of soothing sorrow. Again: he tries to make the soul faint under them—repine and murmur, and charge God foolishly—not to believe his love and wisdom in the furnace. In these ways Satan tries to separate from the love of Christ. A time of tribulation is a time of danger.

(2) *Persecution, famine, nakedness, peril, sword*—all these are weapons which Satan makes use of against God's children. The history of the Church in all ages has been a history of persecution. No sooner does a soul begin to show concern for religion—no sooner does that soul cleave to Jesus, than the world talk, to the grief of those whom God hath wounded. What bitter words are hurled against that soul ! In all ages this has been true: " They wandered about in sheep-skins and goat-skins, being destitute, afflicted, tormented; of whom the world was not worthy." Those that eat the bread of God have often been driven from their quiet meal—those who are clothed with Christ have often had to part with worldly clothing, and have been exposed to famine, nakedness, peril, and

123

sword—the last extremity. Cain murdered Abel. They killed the Prince of Life; and so all his creatures ever since have been exposed to the same. Do not say, The times are changed, and these are the days of toleration. Christ is not changed—Satan is not changed, and, when it suits his turn, he will use the same weapons.

III. *All these cannot separate us.*

" In all these things we are more than conquerors, through Him that loved us."

How are we more than conquerors ?

1. *We conquer even before the battle is done.* In all other battles we do not know how the victory is to turn until the battle is won. In the battle of Waterloo, it was long thought that the French had gained; and Napoleon sent several despatches to Paris, telling that he had won. But in the fight with the world, Satan, and the flesh, we know how the victory is to turn already. Christ has engaged to carry us through. He will guard us against the darts of the law, by hiding us in his blood. He defends us from the power of sin by his Holy Spirit, put within us. He will keep us, in the secret of his presence, from the strife of tongues. The thicker the battle, the closer will he keep to us; so that we can sing already: " I thank God, through Jesus Christ our Lord." We know that we shall overcome. Though the world were a million times more enraged—though the fires of persecution were again to be kindled—though my heart were a million times more wicked—though all the temptations of hell were let loose upon me—I know I shall overcome through him that loved me. When Paul and Silas sang in the low dungeon, they were more than conquerors. When Paul sang, in spite of his thorn, " I will glory in my infirmities," he was more than a conqueror.

2. *We gain by our conflict.* Often a victory is a loss. So it was in that battle in Israel, after the dark night in Gibeah. All Israel mourned, for a tribe was nearly cut off out of Israel; and so, in most victories, the song of triumph is mingled with the sobbings of the widow and orphan. Not so in the good fight of faith. We are more than conquerors. We gain by our enemies. (1) *We cling closer to Christ.* Every wave of trouble for Christ's sake lifts the soul higher

upon the Rock. Every arrow of bitterness shot after the believer makes him hide farther back in the clefts of Jesus. Be content, dear friend, to bear these troubles, which make you cling closer to your Beloved. (2) *They shake us loose from sin.* If ye were of the world, the world would love its own. If the world smiled and fawned upon you, you would lie on its lap. But when it frowns, then Jesus is our all. (3) *Greater is your reward in heaven.* We gain a brighter crown. Be not afraid; nothing shall ever separate you from the love of Christ. O that I could know that you were all in Christ's love— that the arms of Jesus were enfolding you—then I would know that all the hatred of men, and all the policy of hell, would never prevail against you ! "If God be for you, who can be against you ? " If God has chosen you—called you—washed you—justified you—then he will glorify you. O yield to his loving hands, you that are not far from the kingdom of God ! Let him wash you, for then he will carry you to glory.

Dundee, Oct. 30, 1841.

FOLLOW THE LORD FULLY

" But my servant Caleb, because he had another spirit with him, and hath followed me fully, him will I bring into the land whereinto he went; and his seed shall possess it."—NUMB. xiv. 24.

THE children of Israel lay encamped below Mount Sinai for about a year, during which time God gave them the law and the tabernacle. Moving across the desert with the pillar-cloud before them, they soon came to Kadesh-barnea, in the edge of the desert, and on the border of the promised land. Here, by God's direction, they sent twelve spies to search the land, and to bring back word " whether the people were strong or weak, few or many; and what the land is that they dwell in, whether it be good or bad; and what cities they dwell in, whether in tents or in strongholds." (Numb. xiii. 18, 19.) Accordingly the spies searched the land from one end to another, going up by the rocky dells of Hebron, and returning by the pleasant vale of Eshcol. After forty days they returned, bearing a cluster of grapes between two upon a staff; also some pomegranates, and some figs. And as they stood in the midst of assembled Israel, all eyes rested on them—all ears were open to hear their report. The land was good, they said, flowing with milk and honey; but the people were strong, and their cities walled, and very great. Two men alone of the twelve stood boldly forward—Caleb and Joshua; and Caleb said: " Let us go up at once, for we are well able to overcome it." But the people wept that night, and " bade stone Caleb with stones." (Numb. xiv. 10.) And God was angry, and said that the congregation should die in the wilderness. " But my servant Caleb, because he had another spirit with him, and hath followed me fully, him will I bring into the land whereinto he went; and his seed shall possess it." (Verse 24.)

Doctrine. It is a blessed thing to follow the Lord fully.

I. *What it is to follow the Lord fully.*

1. *To follow Christ all our days.*

This was the way with Caleb; he followed the Lord all his days—he followed him fully. We find it recorded of him, forty years after, when he was an old man of eighty-five, that " he wholly followed the Lord God of Israel." He did not follow God for a time, or by fits and starts, but all his days—he followed him fully. *There are many like Lot's wife,* who flee out of Sodom for a while. She was greatly alarmed—the angels laid hands upon her—she heard the words of warning, and fled for a time; but she soon gave up—she looked back, and became a pillar of salt. So, many are awakened, and flee for their life—they weep—pray—seek salvation; but they do not hold out—they are allured by an old companion or a favourite lust, and so they draw back. *Many are like those spoken of in John* vi.: They follow Jesus for a time, and are called his disciples; they hear the gracious words that proceed out of his mouth; but by-and-by some discovery of doctrine or duty is made which offends them: " From that time many of his disciples went back, and walked no more with Jesus." It is those who never go back that follow him fully. *Many are like the Galatians.* When Paul first preached to them, they received him " as an angel of God, even as Christ Jesus." They spoke of the blessedness of being in Christ, and the great salvation. They loved Paul, so that if it had been possible they would have plucked out their own eyes and given them to him (Gal. iv. 15); and yet they did not follow the Lord fully. They were soon removed from the Gospel of Christ to another gospel. " O foolish Galatians, who hath bewitched you ? " And now they hated Paul for speaking the truth to them. So with many of you. This is not following fully. *Many in affliction begin to follow Christ.* (Ps. lxxviii. 34.) When laid on a sick-bed, or when some bereavement occurs, they take to their Bible—begin to weep and pray. But the world comes back upon them—temptation—old companions—and they go back. They do not follow the Lord fully.

Ah ! how many in this congregation are witnesses that ye have not followed the Lord fully. Ye did run well, who did hinder you ? How many of you were impressed ! Divine things appeared great and precious in your eyes—you came to the Lord's table—you sat down with solemnity—and where are you now ? Have you not gone quickly out of the way ? *Those of you who would follow Christ fully all your days, must be like Lot:* Not only flee from Sodom, but flee to Zoar—you must not rest in convictions, however deep. It is a good thing to be awakened, but, ah ! you are not saved. If you would follow Christ fully, you must get fully into Christ. *You must continue in his word:* " Then said Jesus to those Jews that believed on him, If ye continue in my word, then are ye my disciples indeed." (John viii. 31.) Remember, " ye are saved by the Gospel, if ye keep in memory what I preached unto you, unless ye have believed in vain." *You must be like Mary*, who sat at his feet and heard his word. *You must be like aged Simeon:* " Behold, there was a man in Jerusalem whose name was Simeon, the same was just and devout, waiting for the Consolation of Israel." Perhaps he was converted when a young man; but it was no slight work—soon over; he followed the Lord fully all his days; and now, when he was an old man, he was still waiting for the Consolation of Israel. He followed the Lord fully, and now he follows the Lamb in paradise. *You must be like the palm tree:* "The righteous shall flourish like the palm tree; he shall grow like a cedar in Lebanon. Those that be planted in the house of the Lord shall flourish in the courts of our God. They shall still bring forth fruit in old age; they shall be fat and flourishing." (Ps. xcii.) The palm tree and cedar have both this wonderful property, that they are fruitful to the last: and so it is with the living believer—he is a Christian to the last—full of the Spirit, full of love, full of holiness to the last. Like fine wine, the older the better. "The path of the just is like the shining light, which shineth more and more unto the perfect day." *You must be like Paul.* From the day of his conversion, Paul was a new creature. The love of Christ constrained him, and he lived no more unto himself, but unto him that died for him and rose again. We never hear of his slackening his pace, or giving over fighting: "Forgetting the things that are behind, and reaching forth unto the things that are before, I press toward the mark." Even when an old man, he did not lose the fire of his love, or zeal, or compassion: "I am ready to be offered, and the hour of my departure is at hand: I have fought a good fight, I have finished my course, I have kept the faith." He followed the Lord fully: he never looked back—he never halted—he never slumbered—he was a second Caleb. So must you be, if you would be saved. "He that endureth to the end shall be saved." Not he that has a good beginning, but he that follows fully.

2. *To follow Christ with all the heart.*

This was the way in which Caleb followed the Lord—with all his heart—fully. He had no inconsistencies—he followed the Lord in all he did.

(1) *The most of Christians do not follow the Lord fully—the most have some inconsistency.* Most do not reflect Christ's image in every part. The most do not think it attainable—they are discouraged from seeking it. Many do not think it desirable; at least they think it better for the time to have this and that weakness.

Some do not follow Christ in his lowliness. Christ compared himself to the lily of the valleys: " I am the rose of Sharon, and the lily of the valleys." This was to express his lowliness—his genuine humility. Although he had no sin of his own to make him humble, yet he was humble in his own nature. He did not vaunt himself— did not seek the flattery of men. Some do not follow Christ in this. Some who seem really saved persons, yet have this unlikeness to Christ. They are proud—proud of being saved—proud of grace— proud of being different from others. *Some do not follow Christ in his self-denial.* He was rich, yet for our sakes became poor, that we through his poverty might be rich. While we were sinners, Christ died for us. He had not where to lay his head. Yet many who seem to be Christians seek their own comfort and ease before everything else. They do not drink into Christ's Spirit in this. *Some do not follow Christ in his love.* Christ was love. He descended out of love—lay in the manger out of love—lived a life of sinless obedience out of love—died out of love. Yet some who are Christians do not follow him in ˙this—do not love as he loved. Some have little compassion upon sinners—can sit at ease in their own houses, and see a world perish for lack of knowledge. How few will do anything out of love !

(2) *Many Christians have a time of decay.*

So it was with Ephesus. At one time they were " blessed with all spiritual blessings "—" chosen to be holy and without blame before him in love." They were followers of God, as dear children, and walked in love, as Christ loved them. But a time of decay followed, and Christ says: " I have this against thee, that thou hast left thy first love." They were not like Caleb—they did not follow the Lord fully. *So it was with David.* When he fell into gross and open sin, his whole soul seemed to decay for a time, all his bones seemed to be broken, and he feared that God would take away the Spirit from him for ever. He did not follow the Lord fully. *So it was with Solomon.* When Solomon began to reign, it seemed as if he would follow the Lord fully. The Lord appeared to him in Gibeon, saying: " Ask what I shall give thee." " God gave Solomon wisdom and under-standing, exceeding much; and largeness of heart, even as the sand that is on the sea-shore." And God enabled him to build the temple, and blessed him in all things. Yet did Solomon suffer a sad decay: " He loved many strange women. For it came to pass, when Solomon was old, that his wives turned away his heart after other gods: and his heart was not perfect with the Lord his God, as was the heart of David his father." He did not follow the Lord fully. *So it was with Asa:* "Asa did that which was good and right in the sight of the Lord his God." (2 Chron. xiv.) By his faith he overcame the Ethiopian army of a thousand thousand. He also made a covenant, and all Judah rejoiced at the oath. Yet he suffered a sad decay. For, when the king of Israel came against him, his faith failed him. And when he was old, he was diseased in his feet; nevertheless he sought not to the Lord, but to the physicians. He did not follow the Lord fully. *So it was with the five virgins.* They were wise, and took oil with them in their vessels with their lamps; yet while the bridegroom tarried, they all slumbered and slept. They suffered a sad decay. They did not follow the Lord fully.

Ah ! this must not be the way with you, if you would be like Caleb, and follow the Lord fully. You must follow him without any inconsistency, and without any decay.

(1) *You must be like those that say: "I am the Lord's."* " One shall say, I am the Lord's." God says: " My son, give me thine heart." Ye are bought with a price—ye are not your own. If you would be a Caleb, you must give yourself away to him—you must give away your understanding, will, and affections—your body, and all its members—your eyes and tongue—your hands and feet: so that you are in no respect your own, but his alone. Oh, it is sweet to give up yourself to God—to be filled with his Spirit—to be ruled by his Word; a little vessel full of him—a vessel to bear his name— a vessel afore prepared unto glory ! This is to follow the Lord fully.

(2) *You must be changed into the same image.* " We all, with open face, beholding as in a glass the glory of the Lord, are changed into the same image, from glory to glory, even as by the Spirit of the Lord." (2 Cor. iii. 18.) Our foolish hearts think it better to retain some part of Satan's image, but, ah ! this is our happiness, to reflect every feature of Jesus, and that for ever—to have no inconsistency—

to be like him in every part; to love like him—to weep like him—to pray like him—to be changed into his likeness: "I shall be satisfied when I awake with thy likeness."

(3) *You must have his whole law written in your hearts:* "I will put my law in their inward parts, and write it in their hearts." This is your chief happiness, to let every commandment have its proper place in your heart—to have it graven deep there, so that it cannot be effaced. This is to follow the Lord fully.

3. *To follow Christ at all hazards.*

So it was with Caleb. The congregation "bade stone him with stones;" still he did not care, he would do his duty, whatever evil should befall him. He followed the Lord fully. Ah! there are many that follow Christ in the sunshine, that will not follow him in the storm. When the winter comes, the swallows fly away. There are many like the swallows. Many do not follow fully.

(1) *Reproach makes many stagger.* As long as it is fashionable to be religious, and a man's character is advanced by it, rather than otherwise, then many follow Christ; but when it becomes a proverb and a byword, many are offended. Butterflies come out when the sun is warm; but a shower of rain makes them hide. (2) *When men lose their worldly ease.* When Paul and Barnabas were going to Asia, they took John Mark along with them; but when the work appeared dangerous, he went back. (Acts xv. 37.)

If we would follow the Lord fully, we must go through good and bad report.

(1) *We must bear his reproach:* "Let us go out to him without the camp, bearing his reproach." We must bear the reproach even of our nearest friends: "He that loveth father or mother more than me, is not worthy of me; and he that loveth son or daughter more than me, is not worthy of me." We would fain go to heaven without reproach, but it cannot be, if we go the narrow way, and follow Christ fully.

(2) *We must not think of ease if we follow Christ fully.* Christ trod a thorny path: he was crowned with thorns—we must not think to be crowned with roses. Paul says: "For whom I have suffered the loss of all things, and do count them but dung, that I may win Christ."

(3) *We must be willing to lose our life:* "Neither count I my life dear unto myself"—"The time cometh, when whoso killeth you shall think that he doeth God service"—"Whoso findeth his life shall lose it"—"Be faithful unto death"—"They overcame him by the blood of the Lamb and they loved not their lives unto the death."

Oh! it is sweet to follow Christ fully, for then we shall reign with him: "If we suffer with him, we shall reign with him. If we deny him, he will deny us."

II. *How we may be enabled to follow the Lord fully.*

1. *By keeping the eye upon him.* This was what enabled Caleb to follow the Lord fully. He endured as seeing Him who was invisible; he set the Lord always before him. If Caleb had been seeking a name, or his own wealth, fame, or honour, he would not have followed fully—he could not have followed all his days, nor with all his heart, nor at all hazards.

If you would follow Christ fully, you must know him fully. *A sight of his beauty* draws us to follow him. "He is the chief among ten thousand, and altogether lovely." "And I, if I be lifted up, will draw all men unto me." There is an indescribable loveliness in Christ that draws the soul to follow him. All divine perfections dwell in him; and yet he offers to save us. *His suitableness draws us to follow him.* He just answers the need of our soul. We are all guilty—he is all righteousness. We all weakness—he all strength. Nothing can more completely answer our soul than Christ doth. The chickens run under the feathers of their mother when they see them stretched out—the dove flutters into the clefts—Noah into the ark; and our soul thus follows Jesus. *His freeness draws us to follow him.* "He will in no wise cast out." He forgives seventy times seven. It is the keeping the eye on Christ that makes you follow him. It is seeing the King in his beauty that makes the soul cleave to him, and run after him. "My soul followeth hard after thee"—"Run the race set before you, looking unto Jesus."

2. *By having the Holy Spirit.* Caleb "had another spirit." The other spies were carnal men; but Caleb had another spirit—he had the Holy Spirit dwelling in him—leading him—upholding and

132

renewing. So with all who follow the Lord fully. The Spirit of God in the soul is a constant stream—a well of water springing up unto everlasting life. Lot's wife looked back; but she had not the indwelling of the Holy Spirit. It is a filling Spirit—he loves to fill the heart—to fill every chamber. " Be filled with the Spirit "— " Now the God of hope fill you." He loves to write the whole law on the heart—to lift the whole soul to God.

III. *The motives to follow the Lord fully.*

" Him will I bring into the land." The other spies died of the plague—the people fell in the wilderness; but Caleb and Joshua, because they followed the Lord fully, were received into the land.

1. *It is the only happy life.* There is no happier life under the sun than to follow Christ all our days. There is not a more miserable creature on earth than a backslider. Every time we turn aside from following Christ, we are providing misery for ourselves— hidings, desertions, and broken bones. The only happy life is to follow with all our heart. We generally think it is happy to have this or that idol, but we are quite mistaken. Your true happiness is in self-surrender—in giving up your heart and all to him. Any one inconsistency mars your joy—mars communion. Are you not far happier in your times of closest walking with God ? O that it were so with me always ! Decays bring darkness and misery. The only happiness is to suffer the loss of all things. Many Christians are not w li ng to deny themselves—to suffer for Christ's sake—not willing to bear reproach or persecution. Christ will give a hundredfold more—peace of conscience.

2. *This is the way to be useful.* It is the thriving Christian that is the useful Christian—the one that follows Christ fully. The blessing to Abraham was: " I will bless thee, and make thee a blessing." This was eminently true of Paul. He followed Christ fully; and what a blessing he was ! So would you be, if you followed Christ fully. If you bore all the features of Christ about with you, what a blessing would you be to this place, and to the world !— not a cumberer of the ground. How useful to your children and neighbours !

3. *This is the way to die happily.* If you would die the death of Christ's people, you must live their life. Inconsistent Christians generally have a painful death-bed; but those that follow Christ fully can die like aged Paul—" I am ready to be offered; " like Job— " I known that my Redeemer liveth."

4. *This will insure a great reward.* Every man shall be rewarded according as his work has been. Some will be made rulers over five, some over ten cities. I have no doubt that every sin, inconsistency, backsliding, and decay of God's children, takes away something from their eternal glory. It is a loss for all eternity; and the more fully and unreservedly we follow the Lord Jesus now, the more abundant will our entrance be into his everlasting kingdom. The closer we walk with Christ now, the closer will we walk with him to all eternity. " Thou hast a few names in Sardis which have not defiled their garments. They shall walk with me in white, for they are worthy."

Dundee, 1842.

THE RIGHT IMPROVEMENT OF AFFLICTION

" Surely it is meet to be said unto God, I have borne chastisement, I will not offend any more: that which I see not, teach thou me; if I have done iniquity, I will do no more."—JOB xxxiv. 31, 32.

THIS world is a world of trouble: " Man that is born of a woman, is of few days and full of trouble," " We dwell in cottages of clay, our foundation is in the dust, we are crushed before the moth," Job iv. 19. This world has sometimes been called, " a vale of tears." Trials come into all your dwellings; the children of God are not excepted; there is a " need be " that you be in many temptations. " Count it not strange when you fall into divers temptations, as though some strange thing happened unto you." If this be so, of how great importance is it, that you and I be prepared to meet it. The darkest thunder cloud only covers the heavens for a time.

134

" Surely it is meet to be said unto God, I have borne chastisement. I will not offend any more: that which I see not, teach thou me; if I have done iniquity, I will do no more."

From these words, I would desire to show you the right improvement we should make of affliction.

I. The threefold improvement of affliction.

II. The meetness for it.

I. The threefold improvement of affliction.

1. The first improvement of affliction is *submission*. It is the temper of one who justifies God: " I have borne chastisement." This was the feeling of Daniel in the midst of the affliction which God brought on Israel. This is shown in Daniel ix. 7, 8, " O Lord, righteousness belongeth unto thee, but unto us confusion of face," &c.; verse 14, " Therefore hath the Lord watched upon the evil, and brought it upon us; for the Lord our God is righteous in all his works which he doeth: for we obeyed not his voice."

You will notice, then, in all this, that Daniel accepts of the punishment of his iniquity. The same thing you will notice in the 9th chapter of Nehemiah and 33rd verse, " Howbeit thou art just in all that is brought upon us; for thou hast done right, but we have done wickedly." The same thing you will notice in the 26th of Leviticus, 40th verse, " If they shall confess their iniquity, and the iniquity of their fathers, with their trespasses which they have trespassed against me, and that also they have walked contrary unto me." And then, middle of 41st verse, " If then their uncircumcised hearts be humbled, and they then accept of the punishment of their iniquity," &c.; to the end of the chapter. God here says, if they accept of the punishment of their iniquities, he will remember them. Now, this is the first improvement you should make of affliction. How different this from many of you; you do not accept of the punishment of your iniquities; your heart rises against God. 1. In your thoughts. 2. In hard words. The man begins to blaspheme God; he says, God is a tyrant—could God not have spared my child ? This is what is spoken of at the pouring out of the fifth and sixth vials. These are their words in hell; when God pours out his wrath, they will blaspheme him. There is still a third

135

way, and that is in your actions. Your words are not only against God, but your actions are against him. If I could lay bare your hearts, you would see such complaining—such anger against God, that you would see the truth of what I am saying. Remember, it is right to learn contentment. What right have you to complain? What right have you to challenge God's dealings with you? If little children were to take it upon them to decide upon the proceedings of both Houses of Parliament, what would you think of it? And what right have you to challenge God's government? We should say with Job, " The Lord gave, and the Lord hath taken away; blessed be the name of the Lord."

2. The second improvement of affliction is, *humble inquiry into God's meaning:* " What I know not, teach thou me." This is the proper improvement of affliction. This is the way in which Job himself received his trial. Job x. 2, " I will say unto God, Do not condemn me: show me wherefore thou contendest with me." The same you will notice in the 23rd chapter, 3rd verse, " Oh that I knew where I might find him! that I might come even to his seat! I would order my cause before him, and fill my mouth with arguments. I would know the words which he would answer me, and understand what he would say unto me. Will he plead against me with his great power? No; but he will put strength in me. There the righteous might dispute with him; so should I be delivered for ever from my judge." You will notice that Job was to be made acquainted why God dealt thus with him. The same was the case with Joshua, 7th chapter, 6th verse, " And Joshua rent his clothes and fell to the earth upon his face before the ark of the Lord until the eventide, he and the elders of Israel, and put dust upon their heads. And Joshua said, Alas, O Lord God, wherefore hast thou at all brought this people over Jordan, to deliver us into the hand of the Amorites, to destroy us? would to God we had been content, and dwelt on the other side Jordan! O Lord, what shall I say, when Israel turneth their backs before their enemies! For the Canaanites and all the inhabitants of the land shall hear of it, and shall environ us round, and cut off our name from the earth: and what wilt thou do unto thy great name? " When affliction came, Joshua

waited for an explanation. This also seems to have been the case with the apostle Paul when he said, " Lord, what wilt thou have me to do? " Brethren, the opposite of this is very common among you. When God sends affliction into an ungodly family; when God takes away a child, or lays a father on a bed of affliction; do they inquire of God why he did it ? Ah ! you despise the chastening of the Lord. Brethren, it is a fearful thing not to ask God's meaning in affliction. It is his loudest knock, and often his last. The same thing happens with God's children. You have been loving some idol—some secret sin—some secret lust, and God afflicts you. Do you ask an explanation ? The same thing takes place in a church. The members are unholy. Then perhaps he afflicts it as he did Laodicea. Do we seek an explanation ? Ah no ! This is what this town should do in its poverty.

3. There is a third improvement of affliction, that is, *the forsaking of sin:* " I will not offend any more." " If I have done iniquity, I will do no more." God's great design in affliction is to make you forsake your sin: " He that covereth his sins shall not prosper; but whoso confesseth and forsaketh them shall have mercy," Prov. xxviii. 13. This was God's way with Manasseh: so it should be in all affliction. God afflicts you, that you may cast away your sin; you will not hear his voice of mercy; you will not hear his voice of love; but he brings you under the rod, in order to bring you into the covenant. How often does it do the contrary ? I have seen a drunkard afflicted, and he went deeper into sin—farther away from God. " Ephraim is a cake not turned." There are some among you, that remind me of an aged tree that has been struck with lightning, and now stands stript of its leaves, a monument in the earth. So are many of your families. I tell you, brethren, if mercies, and if judgments do not convert you, God has no other arrows in his quiver.

II. The meetness of inquiring into God's reasons of affliction.

1. It is meet, because *it is God that is dealing with you.* This affliction in your family, this affliction with yourself, is from God. " Who hardeneth his heart against God and prospereth ? "

2. It is meet, because *this is God's meaning in your affliction.* God's meaning is, to save the unconverted, and to sanctify his own.

I believe, that every time the sun shines into your dwelling, it is meant to make you turn unto God; and it is the same with affliction; it is meant to make you turn to him; or if you be a child of God, every affliction is meant to make you cast your idols to the moles and to the bats, and to turn to God.

3. It is meet, because *God can destroy.* You know, brethren, that the same hand that afflicts can destroy. The same hand that kindled the burning fever in your breast, can kindle up the flames of hell for you.

ELECTING LOVE

" Ye have not chosen me, but I have chosen you, and ordained you, that ye should go and bring forth fruit, and that your fruit should remain."—JOHN xv. 16.

THIS is a very humbling, and, at the same time, a very blessed word to the true disciple. It was very humbling to the disciples to be told that they had not chosen Christ. Your wants were so many, your hearts were so hard, that ye have not chosen me. And yet it was exceedingly comforting to the disciples to be told that he had chosen them: " Ye have not chosen me, but I have chosen you." This showed them that his love was first with them,—that he had a love for them when they were dead in sins. And then he showed them that it was love that would make them holy: " Ye have not chosen me, but I have chosen you, and ordained you, that ye should go and bring forth fruit, and that your fruit should remain."

Let us take up the truths in this verse as they occur.

I. *Men naturally do not choose Christ,* " Ye have not chosen me." This was true of the apostles; this is true of all that will ever believe to the end of the world. " Ye have not chosen me." The natural

138

ear is so deaf that it cannot hear; the natural eye is so blind that it cannot see Christ. It is true in one sense, that every disciple chooses Christ; but it is when God opens the eye to see him—it is when God gives strength to the withered arm to embrace him. But Christ's meaning is, You would never have chosen me, if I had not chosen you. It is quite true, that when God opens a sinner's heart, he chooses Christ and none but Christ. It is quite true, that a heart that is quickened by the Spirit, ever chooses Christ, and none but Christ, and will forego all the world for Christ. But, brethren, the truth here taught us is this, that every awakened sinner is willing to embrace Christ, but not till made willing. Those of you who have been awakened, you did not choose Christ. If a physician were to come into your house, and say he had come to cure you of your disease, if you felt that you were not diseased, you would say, I have no need of you, go to my neighbour. This is the way you do with Christ: he offers to cure you, but you say you are not diseased; he offers to cover your naked soul with his obedience, you say, I have no need of that covering.

Another reason why you do not choose Christ is, *you see no beauty in him:* " He is a root out of a dry ground, in which there is no form nor comeliness." You see no beauty in his person, no beauty in his obedience, no glory in his cross. You see him not, and, therefore, you do not choose him.

Another reason why you do not choose Christ is, *you do not want to be made holy by him:* " He shall be called Jesus, for he shall save his people from their sins." But you love your sin,—you love your pleasure, therefore when the Son of God comes and says, He will save you from your sin, you say I love my sin,—I love my pleasure. So you can never come to terms with Christ: " Ye have not chosen me;"—Although I died, yet you have not chosen me. I have spoken to you many years, and yet you have not chosen me. I have sent you my Bible to instruct you, and yet you have not chosen me. Brethren, this accusation will meet you in the judgment, I would have covered you with my obedience, but ye would not have me.

II. *Christ chooses his own disciples:* " I have chosen you." Christ looked upon them with a look of divine benignity, and said,

"I have chosen you." Every one whom he brings to glory, he chooses them.

1. *The time when he chose them.* I observe that it was *before they believed:* "Ye have not chosen me, but I have chosen you," as much as to say, I began with you, you did not begin with me. You will notice this in Acts xvii. 9, 10, "Then spake the Lord to Paul in the night by a vision, Be not afraid, but speak, and hold not thy peace: for I am with thee, and no man shall set on thee to hurt thee; for I have much people in this city." Paul was at this time at Corinth, the most lascivious and wicked city in the ancient world; they were given over to banqueting and grievous idolatry, and yet Christ said to Paul, "I have much people in this city." They had not chosen Christ, but he had chosen them; they had not repented, yet Christ fixed his eye on them. This plainly shows you that Christ chooses his own before they seek him.

But, farther, Christ chooses his own *from the beginning*; 2 Thess. ii. 13, "But we are bound to give thanks alway to God for you, brethren, beloved of the Lord, because God hath from the beginning chosen you to salvation through sanctification of the Spirit, and belief of the truth;" Eph. i. 4, "According as he hath chosen us in him before the foundation of the world, that we should be holy and without blame before him in love." So, brethren, it was before the foundation of the world that Christ chose his own; when there was neither sun nor moon; when there was neither sea nor land—it was from the beginning. Ah! he might well say, you have not chosen me. It was before man loved man, or angel loved angel, that Christ chose his own. Now, I know the meaning of Paul when he says, That you may be able to know the length and breadth, the height and the depth of the love of Christ, which passeth knowledge. Now, I am not surprised at the death of Christ! it was a love so great that it broke over the banks that held it in; a love that broke over a Calvary and a Gethsemane. O, brethren, do you know this love?

But I come now to *the reason of his love*—"Ye have not chosen me, but I have chosen you." Now, it is a very natural question, why did he choose me? I answer, that the reason why he chose

140

you was, the good pleasure of his will. You will see this illustrated in Mark iii. 13, " And he goeth up into a mountain, and calleth unto him whom he would: and they came unto him." There was a great crowd round about him: he called some, he did not call all. The reason here given why he did it is, " He called whom he would." There is no reason in the creature; the reason is in him who chooses. You will see this in Malachi i. 2, " I have loved you, saith the Lord; yet ye say, Wherein hast thou loved us ? Was not Esau Jacob's brother ? saith the Lord: yet I loved Jacob, and I hated Esau." Were they not of the same mother ? yet I loved Jacob, and I hated Esau. The only reason given, you see, is, " I will have mercy on whom I will have mercy." You will see this also in Rom. ix. 15, 16. The only reason given in the Bible why Christ loved us—and if you study till you die you will not find another—is, " I will have mercy on whom I will have mercy." This is evident from all those that Christ chooses. We read of two great apostasies—one on earth, the other in heaven. First of all, one in heaven; Lucifer, the sun of the morning, through pride, sinned, and God cast him and those that sinned with him into hell. The second was on earth; Adam sinned, and was driven out of paradise. They were both deserving of punishment. God had a purpose of love. Who is it for ? Perhaps angels pleaded for their fellow-angels; yet Christ passed them by, and died for man. Why did he die for man ? the answer is, " I will have mercy on whom I will have mercy." The same is evident in the individuals Christ chooses. You would think Christ would choose the rich, and yet what says James: " Hath not God chosen the poor of this world rich in faith, and heirs of the kingdom which he hath promised to them that love him? "

Again, you would think Christ would choose the noble; they have not the prejudices that the poor have; but what says the Scripture, " Not many rich, not many noble are called."

Again, you would think he would choose those that are learned. The Bible is written in difficult language; its doctrines are hard to be understood; yet what says Christ, " I thank thee, O Father, that thou hast hid these things from the wise and prudent, and hast revealed them unto babes."

141

Again, you would think he would have chosen the virtuous. Though there are none righteous, yet there are some more virtuous than others; yet what says Christ, The publicans and the harlots enter the kingdom of heaven, while the Pharisee is shut out. " O the depth both of the riches and knowledge of God, how unsearchable are his judgments, and his ways past finding out ! " Why did he take the most vile ? Here is the only reason I have been able to find ever since I read my Bible—" I will have mercy on whom I will have mercy, and I will have compassion on whom I will have compassion."

Christ chooses some that seek him, and not others. There was a young ruler came to Christ, and said, " Good master, what good thing shall I do that I may inherit eternal life ? " He was in earnest, yet something came in the way and he went back. A woman that was a sinner came behind Christ weeping, she also was in earnest, Christ said unto her, " Thy sins which are many are forgiven thee." What made the difference ?—" I will have mercy on whom I will have mercy." " He called unto him whom he would." O, my brethren, be humbled under the sovereignty of God. If he will have compassion, then he will have compassion.

III. But I hasten to the third and last point: " *I have ordained you that ye should go and bring forth fruit, and that your fruit should remain.*" Christ not only chooses who are to be saved, but he chooses the way; and he not only chooses the beginning and the end, he chooses the middle also. " God hath from the beginning chosen you to salvation, through sanctification of the Spirit and belief of the truth." " According as he hath chosen us in him before the foundation of the world, that we should be holy and without blame before him in love;" Eph. i. 4. And in the eighth chapter of Romans it is said, " Whom he did predestinate, them he also called; and whom he called, them he also justified, and whom he justified, them he also glorified." Salvation is like a golden chain let down from heaven to earth; two links are in the hand of God—election and final salvation; but some of the links are on earth—conversion, adoption, &c. Brethren, Christ never chooses a man to believe, and then leap into glory. Ah ! my brethren, how this takes away

142

the feet from all the objections raised against this holy doctrine of election. Some here, perhaps, say, If I am elected, I will be saved, live as I like. No; if you live an unholy life you will not be saved. Some may say, If I am not elected, I will not be saved, do as I like. Whether you are elected or not, I know not, but this I know—if you believe on Christ you will be saved.

Let me ask you, Have you believed on Christ ? Let me ask you another question, Do you bear his whole image ? then you are elected, and will be saved. But are there any here who have not believed on Christ, and who do not live a holy life, then, whatever you think now, you will find it true that you were among those who were passed by.

Ah ! my brethren, those who deny election, deny that God can have mercy. O, it is sweet truth that God can have mercy. There is nothing in the hardness of your hearts that will keep God from having mercy on you. Go away home with this truth, that God can have mercy. " Ye have not chosen me, but I have chosen you."

HIGH TIME TO AWAKE OUT OF SLEEP

" And that, knowing the time, that now it is high time to awake out of sleep: for now is our salvation nearer than when we believed."— Rom. xiii. 11.

In these words, Paul tells believers that it is waking time; and I would just tell you, dear friends, the same. It is high time for you to awake out of sleep. There is a condition among Christians which may be called sleeping; like the ten virgins, they slumber and sleep. Ah ! I fear there are many sleeping Christians among you. It is waking time, believer. Do you know what o'clock it is ? You do not seem to know how near sunrise it is.

I will now show you what it is to be *sleeping Christians*. It is to be one that has come to Christ yet has fallen asleep in sin. Like the Church at Ephesus, they have left their first love: They do not retain that realization of Christ's preciousness—that freshness of believing. They have forgotten the fresh grasp of a Saviour. So it is with some among yourselves. You may have seen your sins; yet you have lost that fresh conviction of sin you once felt so deeply. You do not see such a beauty in Jesus. The more we look at him, just the more would we look again. Earthly things pall upon the taste; but it is not so with things divine—they grow sweeter the more often you use them. So every time you look at Jesus, he grows more precious. The rose is sweet, yet it loses its smell; but the lovely Rose of Sharon grows sweeter and sweeter. Earthly apples lose their taste; but the apple-tree does not so—" Stay me with flagons, comfort me with apples, for I am sick of love." Sleepy Christians, you have lost taste for the apples. O ! it is not time for you to sleep any longer. Believer, if you sleep on, you will soon doubt if ever you have come to Christ at all.

To awake out of sleep, then, is to see that *divine things are realities*. When you are half asleep, you see things imperfectly. Ah ! you are not affected by divine realities. Now, what is it to awaken out of sleep ? To awaken out of sleep is to see sin as it is——your heart as it is—Christ as he is—and the love of God in Christ Jesus. And you can see all this by looking to Calvary's cross. O ! it is an awful thing to look to the cross and not be affected, nor feel conviction of sin—not feel drawn to Christ. O ! I do not know a more sad state than this. O ! pray that you may be wide awake. Dear friends, our life is like a river, and we are like a boat sailing down that river. We are drawing nearer and nearer to the shores of eternity. Some may have believed for forty years. Ah ! your salvation is nearer than when you first believed. Your redemption draweth nigh—the redemption of your whole soul—your complete redemption. And the time is coming when ye will get it—you will be saved, and then the last stone will be put on with shoutings of " Grace ! grace ! unto it." Then will the crown be put upon your heads, for you will be more than conquerors.

144

Dear friends, I do not know how far the day is spent. This is a dark, dark time; but the day is breaking—the shadows are fleeing away. The river Euphrates is drying up—that shows the day is breaking. God is bringing in his ancient people, the Jews, and that shows the day is far spent.

And it is also high time for *unconverted men to awake out of sleep*. O, sinners! you are fast asleep, you are lying dormant—dead. O, sleepy souls! it is high time you should awake, Do you know what angels said when they went to and fro upon the earth? They told the Lord, " Behold, all the earth sitteth still and is at rest." Ah! you are fast asleep. God has given you the spirit of slumber. Do you not remember the message to Amos—" Woe to them that are at ease in Zion "? And that is the case with many of you. When you come to this house, you are in a place where Jesus has called sleepy souls, and where he has been found of very many. O, sleeping souls! it is high time for you to awake. You are living in a dream. Every Christless man will find at last that he has been dreaming. Ah! the time is coming when you shall find that your following after gold is but a golden dream. And is there no pleasure in a dream? Who has not felt that there is pleasure even in dreams. But, ah! you must awake. Like a man condemned to die (and many of you are condemned already), he dreams of home, of his wife and children; of freedom and pleasure; but, ah! he awakes by the toll of the death-bell, and he finds that—behold it was but a dream! Now unconverted men, you are taking a sleep; but, like the man, you will awake from a bright dream to a bitter reality. Dear friends, I often think when I look to your houses as I pass along, and when I look in your faces, that ministers are like watchmen—they see the fire, and they give the alarm. Many of you are in danger as one in a burning house. Sometimes you wonder at our anxiety for you. Sometimes you say, " Why are you so harsh?" Poor soul! it is because the house is on fire! O, then, can we speak too harshly?—can we knock too loudly at the door of your consciences? I remember what a woman once told John Newton on her death-bed: she said, " You often spoke to me of Christ; but O! you did not tell me enough about my danger." O! I fear many of you will tell me the same. O! I fear many may reproach me on a death-bed, or in hell, that I did not tell you more often that there was a hell. Would to God I had none to reproach me at last; God help me to speak to you plainly! It is high time to awake out of sleep, sinner: for now your damnation slumbereth not. Dear friends, it is now more than three years since I first spoke to you, though it just seems like a day since I first came beseeching you to be reconciled to God—beseeching you to come to Jesus. Every day that passes is bringing you nearer to the judgment-seat. Not one of you is standing still. You may sleep; but the tide is going on, bringing you nearer death, judgment, and eternity.

Dear friends, another reason for awaking is *your condemnation is still getting greater and greater*. When I first came among you your guilt was not so great as now. "Despisest thou the riches of his goodness and forbearance, and long-suffering; not knowing that the goodness of God leadeth thee to repentance; but after thy hardness and impenitent heart, treasurest up unto thyself wrath against the day of wrath, and revelation of the righteous judgment of God?"—Romans ii. 4, 5. Do any of you know that you are treasuring up wrath against the day of wrath? You are laying up in the bank. You are laying up wrath for a coming eternity. Will this not convince you that it is high time to awake out of sleep? It is time to-night to put on the Lord Jesus. It is high time, sleeper. It is the very time. Will ye not awake? Ah! I can tell you one thing—you will find it all true at last, that you have treasured up wrath against the day of wrath. Every sin is a drop of wrath; which, like a river dammed up, gets deeper and deeper and fuller till at last it bursts forth. O! are there not many misers of wrath here? Do you not see that it is high time for you to awake out of sleep before you have an infinity of wrath laid up? Awake *now*, and it may be all taken away. There is one ready to take it away if ye will but apply to him. Sinner! awake then.

Another reason is, that *opportunities of awaking are passing away*. Now, I do say there are times of awaking. There is a time when the ark is passing by your houses; and if you allow it to pass, you will find one day, when you would step in, that you will be overcome by the angry waters. You remember the little man of Jericho,

146

Zaccheus. Jesus was passing through Jericho on his way to Jerusalem to be crucified. It was the last time he was to pass that way: it was the last time Zaccheus could see the Saviour. When Jesus was to pass, lest he should be lost among the crowd, he climbed up into a sycamore-tree. Jesus passed, looked up, and said, " Zaccheus, come down, for to-day I must abide at thy house." O ! had he not come down that moment from the sycamore-tree—had he not made haste and come down—he would have come down and gone to a lost eternity. Had he not that hour closed with Jesus, he would have gone to that place where there is no voice of mercy, for Jesus passed by for the last time. And I do say, sinner, if you do not come down from your sycamore-tree, and receive Christ to-night, you may not be permitted to-morrow. Now is the accepted time. O ! come to him *now*. O ! you will rejoice for ever if you entertain him joyfully to-night. Sleepy sinner ! now awake. It is high time to awake; for the time is at hand when there will be no Bible—no more offers of mercy. We have many precious ordinances now; but they will all come to an end. Our Thursday evenings[1] will soon come to an end too. O ! make haste, then, and come down, and Jesus this night will abide in your house. He is saying, " Behold I stand at the door and knock. If any man hear my voice, and open the door, I will come in to him, and will sup with him, and he with me." Had Zaccheus slept, he would never have seen Jesus; and if you do not awake, alas ! alas ! for the day comes when you shall wail because of him.

Dundee, April 2, 1840.

[1] The weekly meeting for prayer and exposition of scripture was held on Thursday evening.

THE SAVIOUR'S TEARS OVER THE LOST

" And when he was come near, he beheld the city, and wept over it,
saying, If thou hadst known, even thou, at least in this thy day,
the things which belong unto thy peace ! but now they are hid from
thine eyes."—LUKE xix. 41, 42.

JESUS Christ is the same yesterday, to-day, and for ever. He is the
same Saviour now that he was that day when he wept over Jerusalem. If he were on earth now as he was then, I have no doubt but
that there are many here to-night over whom he would weep, as he
did over impenitent Jerusalem. I would show you from these words,

I. That the gospel is what belongs to your peace.

II. That there is a day of grace.

III. That Christ is willing and anxious to save sinners.

I. Show *the gospel is what belongs to a man's peace.* " There is no
peace, saith my God, unto the wicked."

1. *It belongs to your peace of conscience.* Sin is the cause of all
sorrow, and the very reason that you are miserable is, because you
are the servant of sin. It is the gospel that first brings peace to an
anxious sinner. In it Christ and his righteousness are set forth, and
it is a saving sight of these that makes the burden fall off a sinner's
back. Those of you who have come to Christ have peace; even in
the midst of raging lusts and temptations, you have peace. When
once we are under grace, we can say, " Sin shall no more have dominion over me." Even when there seems to be no way of escape,
either on this side or on that—even when the world is spreading out
the net to ensnare the soul, still, if the eye be fixed on a living Jesus,
that soul can have peace. None have true peace but those that are
beholding the Lamb of God which taketh away the sin of the world.
Sinner, the gospel, for as much as you despise it, is what belongs
unto your peace. There is no peace out of Christ—there is no peace
and safety here in this world, where Satan's darts are flying so thick,

148

but under the wings of Jesus. No doubt, many have peace who are out of Christ,—they are quite happy, although living under the wrath and curse of God; but what is the reason ? The secret lies in this, they are blind, insensible, spiritually dead. They do not know their own selves. They think they are safe, while, alas ! they are standing on the brink of hell. Oh ! sinner, that is the reason you are so happy; but there is a day coming, when the peace of the most careless, carnal sinner among you, will be eternally broken.

2. *In a time of trouble the gospel peculiarly belongs to your peace.* Man is born to trouble. The past year has proved that in many of your families. There have been many sicknesses, many deaths, and many last farewells among you. Who knows what will take place before this night next year ? The unconverted have got no peace in the hour of trouble,—they have no anchor when the storm rages—no fountain of peace—no covert from the tempest. What an awful and miserable thing it must be, to be without peace when the storm comes. It must surely be an important thing to get into Christ, before trouble, and sickness, and death comes. In truth, the gospel does belong to your peace. All the time I have been among you, I have been offering you peace. If you get Christ, you will get peace; if you never get Christ, you will never get peace. Christ is a covert from every wind. As long as you have no sickness or trouble, you may be stout-hearted, and have a kind of peace; but ah ! what will you do in the hour of your calamity ? " Can thine heart endure, or can thine hands be strong in the days that I shall deal with thee ?

3. *The gospel gives peace at death.* What can give you peace, O sinner, in the hour of death ? Can a neglected Bible give you peace ? Will it comfort you to remember that you have lived contrary to God all your life ? Will you look back with pleasure on your wicked life then ? Will your merry company make you merry then ? Where will all your mirth have gone to in that day ? Will your money avail you in the day of wrath ? What will the end be of those that obey not the gospel ? Will it be peace, sinner ? Ah no ! At present you mock at God's people, and scorn the very thought of conversion, and do you think the end of that will be peace ? You may think so. You may think these things will not make death

terrible; but oh ! sinner, it is just because Satan is blinding your eyes. Sin is the sting of death: yea, these very sins which you now hug in your bosom. Your sweet cup will be poison at death. You think it sweet now; but in the end it will bite like an adder. As sure as you are sitting here to-night, as sure as this year is passing over your heads, so sure will thy sins be turned into the worm that dieth not, and the fire that is never quenched. The judgment is at hand. Does not, then, the gospel belong to your peace ? Some of you will, I believe, remember in the day of your calamity, and when there is no voice of a freely preached gospel in this house, the time when the living water ran clear at your feet, and then, *then* you will confess that these things belong to your peace, when they are for ever hid from your eyes. O sinner, Christ belongs to your peace. He alone can give you peace. He took away the sting of death in his own body. He is our peace. For many a year now, I have been preaching peace to you. I have been a peace-maker. And O, brethren, why is it that you will not receive it ? Why is it that ye do always resist the truth ? Why will ye yet despise Christ and his gospel ? O that you would be wise in time, and give heed unto those things which belong unto your peace.

II. I come now to show you *there is a day of grace.* " If thou hadst known, even thou, at least in this thy day, the things which belong unto thy peace; but now they are hid from thine eyes." The natural day has got its dawn, its noon, and its midnight: so, I believe, has the day of grace. Jerusalem had its dawn, when the prophets stood and told of a coming Saviour. It had its noon, when Jesus stood and cried, " If any man thirst let him come unto me, and drink." And it had its midnight, when he wept over it, and said " If thou hadst known, even thou," &c. The day of grace is that time during which Christ is offered to sinners. With some people that period is equal to their whole lives. They are born under the preaching of the gospel, and they live and die under it. Some divines are of opinion that the day of grace sometimes ends before death; but whether this be true or not, one thing is certain, that there is a gradual hardening of the heart against the work of the Spirit. I have often seen this among you; you grow more hardened the longer you sit and hear the offers of salvation; you become more set upon your idols, and more inclined to follow the devices of your own hearts. I would now mention some of the seasons, which may be called days of grace.

1. *The time of youth.* I do not pretend to give a reason why it is so; but God has so ordered it in his infinite wisdom, that the period of youth is the best time for being saved. It has been observed, and it is very remarkable, that in all the great revivals that have taken place in our own and in bygone days, the most of those who have been converted were young people. Jonathan Edwards states this in his narrative of the revival in New England, and Robe states the same in his, of the revival at Kilsyth in 1742. And have we not seen it among ourselves, that while young persons have been melted and converted, those who are older have only grown more hardened in sin. O young people, improve, I entreat you, your young days. Seek the Lord while yet your hearts are young and tender. If you delay, you will grow harder, and then, humanly speaking, it will be more difficult to be saved. No doubt God can save sinners at any age; but he seems peculiarly to choose the time of youth. He loves to hear an infant sing—he loves to hear praise from the mouths of babes and sucklings. Oh ! then, my brethren, will you not seek him in the days of your youth; will you not call upon him while he may be found ? If you let your young days pass over your heads without being saved, you will remember your misspent privileges when you are in hell, and you will bitterly mourn over them throughout all eternity.

2. *The time of a gospel ministry.* This also may be called a peculiar day of grace. God is very sovereign in giving and taking away this. Sometimes he sends a living ministry to a place, and then a dead one. I have observed this frequently. Jerusalem had its day of faithful preaching. For many a long year did the prophets come preaching peace. Often did God send his messengers, rising early and sending them. Often did Jesus stand in the midst of the unbelieving Jews, offering them peace, preaching to them the gospel of the kingdom; then were there days of grace, but ah ! they did not know it, now they are hid from their eyes. And you too who are

151

now before me, have had your day of grace. Will you let it pass away unimproved ? O sinner, will you enter upon another year with God's wrath hanging over your head ? O is it not an awful thing to let year after year pass over you, and yet remain unsaved? A few hours more now will close this year, and you do not know if ever you will see the close of another one. The last enemy may have come to many of you, and you called to give in your account before this night twelve months. Oh ! sinner strive to enter in.

3. *The time when the Holy Spirit is poured out on a place,* is a peculiar day of grace. At such a time there are many pressing into the kingdom. " The kingdom of heaven suffers violence, and the violent take it by force." It seems easier, humanly speaking, to be saved at such a time as that. Brethren, you have had such a time, and it was an easy matter for you to be saved, that year when I was away from you; but ah ! many of you let it pass by. It may indeed be said of many here, " The harvest is past, the summer is ended, and we are not saved." O brethren, you have been a highly favoured people; but remember these days of gospel mercies will soon be gone, never more to return, and if they leave you unsaved, O what miserable wretches must you be throughout eternity ! You may never see such a time again, as you saw here in the autumn of 1839.[1] Oh! if you would be but wise, and know the day of your merciful visitation.

III. I come now to shew you, that *Christ is willing to save even the hardest of sinners.* " And when he was come near, he beheld the city, and wept over it," &c. Christ here gives two proofs that he is willing to save sinners. 1. His tears; and 2. His words. These were the tears of one who never wept but in reality; and these were the words of one who never spake but in reality. It is impossible for him to lie. " O if thou hadst known," he said. It was a broken wish. It shows a feeling of the greatest love and tenderness. His bowels were yearning with tenderness within him, for the love he bore to their souls. His desire was a true desire. He saw them lying in their sin. They had slain the prophets, and despised their messages.

---

[1] Referring to the revival which broke out in St. Peter's under the ministry of William Burns while he was abroad on the Mission to the Jews.

152

He saw that they would soon crucify himself. He saw their hands red with his own blood; and yet, for all that, he wept over them. He saw the judgments that were coming on them. He saw that they would soon lie down in hell; and therefore he wept, and cried, " O if thou hadst known, even thou, at least in this thy day, the things which belong unto thy peace ! but now they are hid from thine eyes." I believe there are some here to-night, over whom Christ says the same. He sees that you have sinned, against light, and against love; and that you have resisted the Holy Spirit these fifty-two Sabbaths which have now gone over your heads. He sees how you have withstood every warning, how you have resisted his ministers, how you have resisted and crucified the Son of God afresh, how you have wounded Christ in the house of his friends; and yet he says, " O if thou hadst known." Perhaps, sinner, you will not turn, perhaps you will perish, and before another year has passed, you may lift up your eyes in hell, being in torments. He that cannot lie says, he would you were saved; and if you perish, sinner, your blood be on your own head. It is the very essence of the gospel that Christ is willing to save. " He willeth not that any should perish, but that all should come to him and live." Some will say, why did he not save Jerusalem, if he was willing ? To this I answer, that you must take the gospel as you find it. It is not your business nor mine to inquire into anything of the sort. It is sufficient for us to know that he is willing to save. He said, " If any man thirst, let him come unto me and drink," and, again, " Him that cometh unto me I will in no wise cast out."

Now brethren, in conclusion, I beseech you, strive to enter in at the strait gate. Many have entered, why not you ? It may be you have seen your parents, or your children, or your wife, or your husband entering in, and oh ! why should not you? If you would be wise, strive to enter in. Will you let this night go by, and will you enter upon another year, with an unsaved soul. You may never sit in these pews again, and yet will you despise the message still. Ye know not what you do. O brethren, it is a wonder I can stand and look upon you sitting there, with dry eyes. Bethink yourselves in time. Are you still content to remain children of wrath, enemies of God, and heirs of hell ? " O that my head were waters, and mine eyes a fountain of tears, that I might weep day and night for the slain of the daughter of my people !"

Dundee, Dec. 31, 1841.

CONVERSION

" And he shewed me Joshua the high priest standing before the angel of the Lord, and Satan standing at his right hand to resist him. And the Lord said unto Satan, The Lord rebuke thee, O Satan, even the Lord that hath chosen Jerusalem, rebuke thee: is not this a brand plucked out of the fire ?"—Zech. iii. 1, 2.

THE conversion of a soul is by far the most remarkable event in the history of the world, although many of you do not care about it. It is the object that attracts the eyes of the holy angels to the spot where it takes place. It is the object which the Father's eye rests upon with tenderness and delight. This work in the soul is what brings greater glory to the Father, Son, and Spirit, than all the other works of God. It is far more wonderful than all the works of art. There is nothing that can equal it. Ah ! brethren, if you think little of it, or laugh at it, how little have you of the mind of God ?

Conversion may be looked at from different points. The world can notice conversion. They see a young man, perhaps, who was careless like themselves, taking to his closet. They observe a change in his speech. They see a change in his company, and they say it is a whim. There is another view of it which God's children take. They see a soul cast out into the open field to the loathing of its person, and they see Jesus, the glorious Redeemer, stooping down and binding up its wounds. They see a sister, a brother born for eternity. A third view of conversion is as a victory of Christ over the devil—" Is not this is a brand plucked out of the fire ?" The world is a great battle-field. " I will put enmity between thee and the woman, and between thy seed and her seed, it shall bruise thy head, and thou shalt bruise his heel." Satan has the world bound in strong fetters. The whole world lies in the wicked one—lies in his arms, sung to sleep with his lullaby. But there is a great One gone forth, sitting on a white horse, and having on his head many crowns, and ever and anon he is cutting the strong chains with which sinners are bound, and saying, as he does so, to Satan, " Is not this a brand plucked out of the fire? "

I desire, dear friends, by the help of the Holy Spirit, to show you two things from these words.

I. That Satan resists every conversion.

II. That Christ is the advocate of those he saves.

I. Verse 1, " And he showed me Joshua the high priest standing before the angel of the Lord, and Satan standing at his right hand to resist him." There is no doubt but that this passage describes a vision which Zechariah saw, and that Joshua represents Jerusalem. Accordingly, Zechariah saw Joshua as a sinner awakened, and coming and standing before the Lord; but he saw another standing at his right hand to resist him, not an angel of light, but an angel of darkness. Now, brethren, this describes the case of every awakened and converted soul. When God convinces a soul of sin, he brings him to stand before him—then Satan comes to resist him. Before conversion, the devil tries to keep you secure, he cries out peace, peace. He fills you with high notions about yourself. He fills you with pride, and with high notions about your knowledge—that you know your catechism—that you are acquainted with the doctrines of the Bible. Or he binds you with silken fetters to some unlawful attachment—to some one who is going down the broad way, and he makes you to hate the gospel. Or he brings you under the faithful preaching of the gospel and makes you content to sit and hear it, and even delight in hearing it, thereby making you imagine you are Christ's, when you know him not. But the moment Christ comes and awakens you, then comes Satan to resist you. This resistance of Satan is twofold.

1. *He resists you at the bar of God.* In ancient courts of justice the accuser stood at the right hand of the judge, and brought against the accused all his crimes. So is it with Satan. You will see this in Rev. xii. 10, " Now is come salvation, and strength, and the kingdom of our God, and the power of his Christ: for the accuser of our brethren is cast down, which accused them before our God day and

night." The same you will see alluded to in Ps. cix. 6, " Set thou a wicked man over him, and let Satan stand at his right hand." So that you will observe, from the first moment that a spark of grace is put into your heart, Satan stands at the bar of God to accuse you. And what does he accuse you of ? First, he accuses you of sin. He says, That soul is the vilest in the world. Yea, there is none like it. Or sometimes he accuses you of unbelief. That soul has denied thee. Or sometimes he accuses you of going back after you had been awakened. That soul was awakened and has gone back; even after you visited that soul, it went back.

2. *At the bar of conscience.* He says to the sinner, How can you come, you are too vile ?—thou art the chief of sinners, there is none like thee. Or sometimes he says, It is too late; you might have been saved had you come sooner. You might have been saved had you come in youth. Or you might have been saved had you come when you were awakened, but now it is of no use to try, it is too late. Or sometimes he takes another plan. When you are awakened and stand before the angel, he stirs up corruption within you; even when you are upon your knees he stirs up corruption in order to shut your eye from seeing the mercy seat. He stirs up the sin that is in your heart. He makes you to see its vileness in order to keep you away from Christ.

Learn two lessons from this.

1. Learn that *it is a solemn thing to be under conviction of sin.* It is true, you are seeking Christ, but it is also true that Satan is ready to resist you. Do not think you are safe because you are under conviction. Remember you are not saved because you have got a sight of your sins. It is not every awakened sinner that is a saved man. And if it is a solemn thing to be awakened, what must be the danger of those of you who are not awakened ! who are not seeking Christ, who are asleep over hell ! You are in greater danger this day than ever you were, for you are now asleep. You are nearer hell now than ever. You may have sought pardon once, but now you have given over seeking it, and every hour is bringing you nearer hell.

2. A second lesson for those who are under real conviction. Remember *it is only Satan that resists you.* God does not resist you.

156

Christ does not resist you. The Holy Ghost does not resist you. Remember, whoever says your sins are too many to be forgiven, it is not God, it is not Christ. It is Satan. Christ invites you to come to him. The Holy Spirit invites you, and all the friends of Christ invite you. Do not be driven back.

II. Verse 2, " And the Lord said unto Satan, The Lord rebuke thee, O Satan; even the Lord that hath chosen Jerusalem, rebuke thee: is not this a brand plucked out of the fire? " " If any man sin, we have an advocate with the Father, Jesus Christ the righteous." Christ is the advocate of every one he saves, and not only is he an advocate after conversion, but before, and throughout conversion. He answers Satan's objections. There are two arguments here by which he answers Satan. The first is *the free election of God.* Jerusalem was the chief city in the world for wickedness. They had sinned against light, against love, against long-suffering mercy. Yet Christ chose it. He might say, Grant that it is the chief for wickedness, yet God hath chosen it. Grant that that soul is the chief of sinners, yet the Lord is sovereign. " I will have mercy on whom I will have mercy and I will have compassion on whom I will have compassion." This is the argument of Christ. Is it not strange that the very argument which troubles souls is the one which Christ uses as the reason why you should be saved ? Let Satan say, you have sinned against light, against conviction, against love; still, " the Lord that hath chosen Jerusalem rebuke thee: is not this a brand plucked out of the fire? " This shuts Satan's mouth,—this is an argument which he cannot answer. The second argument Christ employs is, *The brand is already plucked out of the fire.* Christ here says, whatever that sinner may have been, he is now plucked out of the fire. And thus all Satan's arguments are urged in vain. All unconverted souls are in the fire. You are in the fire for two reasons,

1. *You are condemned to the fire.* " He that believeth not is condemned already." There is as it were a great pile of wood on which you are placed, and it is set on fire. The fire indeed has not yet reached you though soon it will.

2. A second reason is, *your hell is already begun.* Just as the children of God have their heaven begun, so you have got your hell

begun. You have burning lusts, and burning passions raging within you,—these are the beginnings of hell, But ah! brethren, those of you who have been brought to Christ, are brands plucked out of the fire. Observe that Christ plucks the brands out of the fire, and grafts them into the living vine that they may be made to glorify God by bearing fruit. You will be made to glorify God in one of two ways; either by bearing fruit, or by being cast, soul and body, into hell. " For the Lord hath made all things for himself, even the wicked for the day of evil." O! brethren, which do you choose ? O brands in the fire will you not cry to be plucked out of the fire ! And if Christ do it, will he not have this answer to make to Satan ? " The Lord rebuke thee, O Satan: is not this a brand plucked out of the fire? "

In conclusion, I would just say that this congregation may be divided into two parts: those who are brands over the fire, and those who have been plucked out of the fire. O brands in the fire, will you not cry to be plucked out of the fire ? When he is plucking brands out of the fire beside you, will you not say, Lord, pluck me out of the fire.

Sabbath, May 8, 1842

GRIEVE NOT THE HOLY SPIRIT

" Grieve not the holy Spirit of God, whereby ye are sealed unto the day of redemption."—EPH. iv. 30.

THE unconverted do not like to hear much about the Holy Spirit. "The world cannot receive him because it seeth him not, neither knows him." Unconverted ministers do not often like to preach about the Holy Spirit. Unconverted hearers do not often like to hear about the Holy Spirit. How very foolish to many must such a command as this appear to be. If it had been said, Grieve not a father or a mother, you could have understood it, but when it says, "Grieve not the Holy Spirit," you do not know its meaning.

Paul is here advising Christians to let no vile communications proceed out of their mouth and the argument he uses is one of the most wonderful that ever proceeded from the pen of man. It is, " Grieve not the Holy Spirit whereby ye are sealed unto the day of redemption."

From these words, consider

I. The holy friendship of the Spirit.

II. Some of the ways in which we may grieve this friend.

III. Apply.

J. Then let me shew you *the holy friendship that subsists between the Holy Spirit and a believer's soul.* It is implied in the words, " Grieve not the Holy Spirit," it is only a friend we can grieve. If he was an enemy he would rejoice if we fell. And this shews that he is a true friend, because when we fall the Holy Spirit is grieved. It is quite true that the infinite God does not grieve in the same sense as we do, for that would imply that he was not infinitely happy; but it is quite as true that there is something analogous between his grief and ours.

1. *The Holy Spirit comes and dwells in a believer's heart.* " I will put my Spirit within you, and cause you to walk in my statutes, and ye shall keep my judgments and do them," Ezek. xxxvi. 27. And so the Lord Jesus says in the 14th of John, 16th verse, " I will pray the Father, and he will give you another Comforter, that he may abide with you for ever, even the Spirit of truth; whom the world cannot receive, because it seeth him not, neither knoweth him." And accordingly the apostle Paul says in 1 Cor. vi. 19, " What ! know ye not that your body is the temple of the Holy Ghost which is in you, which ye have of God." And in like manner we find God saying in Leviticus xxvi. 12, " I will walk among you, and will be your God and ye shall be my people." And again he says, " This is my rest, here will I stay for I have desired it." O my brethren, what an intimate friendship this is. Can any friendship be compared with this? Another friend may dwell in our neighbourhood, he may dwell in our family; but ah ! here is a friend that dwells in us.

159

Can there be greater friendship than this ? When the Lord Jesus came from heaven and dwelt among us—when he dwelt with Martha, and Mary, and Lazarus—when he sat down to meat in the Pharisee's house and permitted the woman that was a sinner to wash his feet with her tears, and to wipe them with the hairs of her head:—*that* was friendship. But it was still greater friendship for the Holy Spirit to come and dwell in a clay cottage, the walls of which are covered over with leprosy; and this is the friendship of the Holy Spirit to a believing soul.

2. *The Holy Spirit teaches believing souls.* This is his great office. See John xvi. 12, " I have yet many things to say unto you, but ye cannot bear them now. Howbeit when he the Spirit of truth is come he will guide you into all truth." Then 1 John iii. 20, " But ye have an unction from the Holy One, and ye know all things." Verse 27, " But the anointing which ye have received of him abideth in you; and ye need not that any man teach you." Now, brethren, there is no greater mark of friendship, than to teach one—to bear with a slow scholar. This is the friendship of the Holy Spirit to a believing soul. There can be no greater condescension than for a man of gigantic mind to teach a child the alphabet. It was great condescension in Christ to teach the people when he sat in the boat by the side of the lake. But it is greater friendship when the Holy Spirit comes and teaches you all things; it is greater friendship when he bears with your stupidity, and when he opens your hearts to receive the truth in the love of it. This is friendship.

3. *He teaches the believer to pray;* yea, he prays in the believer. See Rom. viii. 15, " Ye have not received the spirit of bondage again to fear; but ye have received the Spirit of adoption, whereby we cry, Abba, Father." Verse 25, " Likewise the Spirit also helpeth our infirmities;—(the Greek word is very remarkable, He helps our infirmities by coming under the burden) for we know not what we should pray for as we ought; but the Spirit itself maketh intercession for us with groanings which cannot be uttered. And he that searcheth the heart (that is the Lord) knoweth what is the mind of the Spirit, because he maketh intercession for the saints according to the will of God." And the same thing you are taught in the little

epistle of Jude, 20th verse, " But ye, beloved, building up yourselves on your most holy faith, praying in the Holy Ghost." So, brethren, this is another mark of the Holy Spirit's friendship, that he not only dwells in the soul, but he teaches the soul to say, " Abba "—he teaches the soul to " pray in the Holy Ghost." It is true friendship to teach one another to pray. It is a believing mother's part to teach her little children to pray. But the Holy Spirit's love is greater than this, he not only puts the words in our mouth, but he puts the desire in our heart. It is great friendship to pray together: but oh ! it is greater friendship to pray in one, and this is the friendship of the Spirit of God.

4. *He seals the believing heart.* Read the text, " Grieve not the Holy Spirit of God, whereby ye are sealed unto the day of redemption." And again, in the first chapter of the same book, 13th verse, " In whom ye also trusted, after that ye heard the word of truth, the gospel of your salvation; in whom also, after that ye believed, ye were sealed with that Holy Spirit of promise." You know, my brethren, the effect that one's habits have over others, that often the colour of the life is taken from those among whom we live. And you cannot be in the company of a holy man without receiving your impressions from him. But how much more an impression does the Spirit make: it is like the mark that the seal makes on the wax, and it is to the day of redemption, and cannot be broken, if we are sealed with the Holy Spirit of promise.

And now, brethren, let me ask, Do you know anything of this friend ? The world cannot receive him; if you are of the world, you cannot receive him. Do you know anything of the Spirit making groanings within you which cannot be uttered ? Nothing. Then, dear friends, you are far from God. " The world cannot receive him, neither knoweth him." How do you feel at the question ? What ! do you think it foolishness ? " The natural man receiveth not the things of the Spirit of God; for they are foolishness unto him: neither can he know them: for they are spiritually discerned," 1 Cor. ii. 14. If you do not mind these things, the reason is, you are a friend of the world, and will perish with the world.

II. *The ways in which the Spirit may be grieved.* When Christ was on earth, we are told that on one occasion he looked round on the Pharisees, being grieved at the hardness of their hearts. Now, what Jesus then felt, the Holy Spirit feels at the sight of sin. We are told that when Christ looked on Peter, he wept. We are not told what kind of a look it was, but no doubt it was one of grief— no doubt his eye said, Did I deserve this, Peter? Did I deserve that thou shouldest act thus? Have I been an enemy to thee, Peter? Have I ever offended thee, Peter? No doubt this was what his eye said.

But let me mention some of the ways in which the Spirit may be grieved:

1. *By putting the Spirit's work in the place of Christ's work.* The office of the Spirit is to glorify the work of Christ. " He shall glorify me; for he shall receive of mine, and shall show it unto you. All things that the father hath are mine: therefore said I, that he shall take of mine, and shall show it unto you," John xvi. 14, 15. This is the office of the Spirit. He delights not to show himself, but Christ. When the three thousand were converted on the day of Pentecost, it was the Spirit that did it, he showed them the divine excellency of the work of Christ. And why does he this? Because it gives glory to God in the highest, peace on earth, and good will to men. But sometimes, a believer looks away from the work of Christ to the work of the Spirit in him, and he begins to rest on that as the ground of peace. Now, this grieves the Spirit. If he were a selfish Spirit, he would rejoice at this; but he is not a selfish Spirit, and, therefore, nothing grieves him so much as this. " Grieve not the Holy Spirit of God, whereby ye are sealed unto the day of redemption."

2. *When you do not lean all on him.* When you do not take all your holiness from him. This is the great work of the Spirit in you, to make you holy. " Thy Spirit is good, lead me to the land of uprightness." God promises in Ezekiel, " I will put my Spirit within you, and cause you to walk in my statutes, and ye shall keep my judgments and do them." Ezek. xxxvi. 27. Now, as long as you lean on the Spirit for holiness, you and he are friends, but the moment you cease to lean on him, you grieve him. Suppose you were to cross

some deep and rapid stream with one who was much stronger and abler to stand against it than you, and he said, Lean on me when you cross. Now, when you came to the middle of the stream, if you were to say, I cannot lean, and began to swim yourself, would you not grieve your friend ? Now, this is the way in which we grieve the Spirit; for he has said, " Even to your old age I am he; and even to hoar hairs will I carry you," Isa. xlvi. 4. Now, when temptations and trials, and lusts come crowding in, if we do not lean upon the Spirit, we grieve him. Or if we lean upon another. If you lean upon your education, your good resolutions, your past experiences. Or, suppose, you run into temptation, and say, I was well brought up, I am able to resist it. In these ways you grieve the Spirit.

3. *You grieve the Spirit when you do not follow his leadings.* You remember, when Christ was on earth, he said to his disciples, " Follow me." He would have been grieved if they had not followed him. It is so with the other Comforter; he leads us to the wilderness —he sometimes causes groanings within us. Do you resist prayer at such a time ? then you grieve the Spirit. Do you go into temptation against the strivings of your conscience ? then you grieve the Spirit. When he sees you run into temptation, he warns you—he pricks your heart and yet you go. Ah ! in this way you grieve the Spirit.

4. *You grieve the Spirit by despising ordinances.* Ordinances are the channels through which the Holy Spirit pours all blessings into the believing heart. Do you despise ordinances ? then you grieve the Holy Spirit. Suppose you agreed to meet a friend at a certain time; if you were not to go, would you not grieve that friend ? Now, this is just the way in which you grieve the Spirit, when you do not go to ordinances. How many of you come to the meeting on Thursday evenings ? Are there not some who slight the friendship of the Spirit ? Ah ! you will yet feel the disadvantage of it to your own soul.

III. Application.

1. *To those here who have grieved the Spirit.* I am deeply persuaded that many here have grieved the Spirit in a remarkable manner. Does he deserve this at your hand ? Has he ever been a wilderness

163

to you, or a land of darkness ? " Do ye thus requite the Lord, O foolish people and unwise ? is he not thy father that hath bought thee ? hath he not made thee and established thee ? " Deut. xxxii. 6. Do ye provoke the Lord the Spirit to jealousy ? Consider how ungrateful it is to grieve him. Consider what he has done for thee. Did he not convince you of sin ? Has he not breathed upon your soul like the gentle gales of wind from the south ? Is it not then ungrateful so to grieve him ?

Consider, how in grieving the Holy Spirit *you have lost your peace with God*. I have often told you, that you cannot live in sin, and retain peace. " There is no peace, saith the Lord, unto the wicked." You have a guilty conscience; and a guilty conscience cannot come into his presence. Return, sinner.

You will go deeper into sin. " Without me ye can do nothing; " —you cannot resist temptation—you cannot resist self—you cannot overcome sin. O unholy quenchers of the Spirit ! where is this to end you ? The Holy Spirit ebbs out of your heart, and leaves you, like a stranded vessel, dry upon the land. Return.

2. I would say *to those who are receiving the refreshing gales of the Spirit*, Grieve him not; walk softly with this friend. When he draws, run after him. Above all, follow his warnings. When he says, Do not go with this companion, go not with him. When he says, Go not into that path, go not. " Thou shalt hear a voice behind thee saying, This is the way, walk ye in it, when ye turn to the right hand, and when ye turn to the left." Happy souls that grieve not the Holy Spirit. Soon he shall fill that soul, and leave nothing in it but himself. Soon we shall be like him, for we shall see him as he is.

Sabbath, August 7, 1842.

FUTURE PUNISHMENT ETERNAL[1]

" Where their worm dieth not, and the fire is not quenched."—MARK
ix. 44.

IT is very interesting to notice who they are in the Bible that speak
about hell. Now, some think that speaking about hell is not
preaching the gospel; and others think that simple men have no
right to speak of it. Now, to them who think it is not gospel
preaching, I say, it is the truth—the word of God; and to them who
say it is not right to speak about it, I would have them to notice who
it is that speaks most about it. Let us consider,

    I. The persons in the Bible that speak most about hell.

    II. Why these persons speak so plainly of hell.

    III. The names given to hell.

    IV. The hell spoken of in the Bible is not annihilation.

    V. This eternal hell is closed in and surrounded by the attributes
of God.

    I. Let us consider the persons in the Bible that speak about hell.
And the first I would mention is David. He was a man after God's
own heart, yet he speaks of hell. He who wrote the Psalms, the
sweet Psalmist of Israel; he who was filled with love to men, and
love to God; yet hear what he says about hell: " The sorrows of hell
compassed me about," Psalm xviii. 5. Again, " The sorrows of
death compassed me about, and the pains of hell gat hold upon
me," Psalm cxvi. 3. And hear of his deliverance: " And thou hast
delivered my soul from the lowest hell," Psalm lxxxvi. 13. And he

---

[1] It would seem as M'Cheyne's ministry drew toward its sudden close that
the future of the unconverted and the reality of eternal judgment was more
urgently than ever brought before the minds of his hearers. In the last nine
months of his ministry he preached at least four times on hell to his own
congregation. It was also the burden of his last message in Andrew Bonar's
church at Collace—" a sermon so solemn that one said it was like a blast of
the trumpet that would awaken the dead."

tells us also of the fate of the ungodly that will not accept Christ: "The wicked shall be turned into hell, and all the nations that forget God," Psalm ix. 17. "Upon the wicked he shall rain snares, fire, and brimstone, and an horrible tempest; this shall be the portion of their cup," Psalm xi. 6. "Let death seize upon them, and let them go down quick into hell," Psalm lv. 15. Now, whatever you think of the propriety of speaking about hell, David did not think it wrong, for he sang about it.

The next person I would mention is Paul. He was filled with the love of Christ, and he had great love to sinners. Surely that love wherewith God loved Jesus was in Paul. He loved his enemies; notice, when he stood before Agrippa, what his feelings were, "I would to God that not only thou, but also all that hear me this day, were both almost and altogether such as I am, except these bonds," Acts xxvi. 29. He wished them to have the same love—the same joy—the same peace—the same hope of glory. Now Paul never mentions the word hell. It seemed as if it were too awful a word for him to mention; yet hear what he says, "What if God, willing to show his wrath, and to make his power known, endured with much long suffering the vessels of wrath fitted to destruction," Rom. ix. 22. "For many walk, of whom I have told you often, and now tell you, even weeping, that they are the enemies of the cross of Christ, whose end is destruction," Phil. iii. 18. "For when they shall say, peace and safety, then sudden destruction cometh upon them." 1 Thess. v. 3. "The Lord Jesus shall be revealed from heaven with his mighty angels, in flaming fire, taking vengeance on them that know not God, and that obey not the gospel of our Lord Jesus Christ, who shall be punished with everlasting destruction from the presence of the Lord, and from the glory of his power," 2 Thess. i. 7–9. Do not these show you, brethren, that they that have most love in their hearts speak most of hell.

The next person I would speak of is John, the beloved disciple. He had leaned on Jesus' bosom at the last supper, and drawn love out of his bosom. His character was love. You will notice how affectionately his Epistles are written. He addresses them, "beloved," "little children." Yet he speaks of hell; he calls it, seven times over " the bottomless pit "—the pit where sinners shall sink through all eternity. He calls it " the great winepress of the wrath of God," Rev. xiv. 19. But John has got another name for hell, " the lake of fire," Rev. xx. 14. It had often been called " hell; " but it was left for John, the beloved disciple, to call it " the lake of fire."

The next person I shall mention is the Lord Jesus himself. Although he came from God, and " God is love," though he came to pluck brands from the burning, yet he speaks of hell. Though his mouth was most sweet, and his lips like lilies, dropping sweet smelling myrrh—though " the Lord God had given him the tongue of the learned, that he should know how to speak a word in season to him that is weary; " though he spake as never man spake—yet he spoke of hell. Hear what he says, " Whosoever shall say, thou fool, shall be in danger of hell fire," Matt. v. 22. But I think the most awful words that ever came from his lips were, " Ye serpents, ye generation of vipers, how can ye escape the damnation of hell," Matt. xxiii. 33. Again, " Depart from me, ye cursed, into ever-lasting fire," Matt. xxv. 41. And he speaks of it in some of his parables, too: " The angels shall come forth, and sever the wicked from among the just, and shall cast them into the furnace of fire; there shall be wailing and gnashing of teeth," Matt. xiii. 49, 50. And he repeats the words of our text three times over. And could anything be plainer than the words in Mark: " He that believeth not shall be damned."

II. Let us consider, dear brethren, why these persons speak so plainly of hell.

1. *Because it is all true.* Christ is the faithful and true witness. Once he said, " If it were not so, I would have told you." Once he said to Pilate, " Every one that is of the truth heareth my voice." He himself is " the truth." " It is impossible for God to lie." When Jesus appeared on earth, he came with love; he came to tell sinners of hell, and of a Saviour to save from hell; and how could he keep it back ? He saw into hell, and how could he not speak of it ? He was the faithful witness; so it was with David, Paul, and John. Paul said, he had kept nothing back—he had not shunned to declare

167

all the counsel of God. Now, how could he have said that, if he had not spoken of hell as he did ? So must ministers. Suppose I never were to mention hell again, would that make it less tolerable ? Oh, it is true ! it is true; it is all true; and we cannot but mention it.

2. A second reason why they spoke so much of hell was, *because they were full of love to sinners.* They are the best friends that do not flatter us. You know, beloved, Christ's bosom flowed with love. Out of love he had not where to lay his head; out of love he came to die; out of love, with tears he said, " O Jerusalem, Jerusalem, thou that killest the prophets and stonest them which are sent unto thee, how often would I have gathered thy children together, even as a hen gathereth her chickens under her wings, and ye would not ! " Matt. xxiii. 37. And with the same breath he said, " How can ye escape the damnation of hell ?" So it was with Paul: " Knowing therefore the terror of the Lord, we persuade men," 2 Cor. v. 11. Paul could weep over sinners; he says, " For many walk of whom I have told you often, and now tell you, even weeping, that they are the enemies of the cross of Christ," Phil. iii. 18. His tears fell on the parchment as he wrote. O ! if we had more love to you, we would tell you more about hell. They do not love you that do not warn you, poor hell-deserving sinners. O ! remember that love warns.

3. A third reason why they spoke so plainly of hell, was, *that they might be free from blood-guiltiness.* Jesus did not want your blood laid at his door, therefore he spoke of the " furnace of fire," and of " the worm that dieth not." Ah ! he says, " How often would I have gathered you, but you would not ! " God would not have blood-guiltiness laid to his charge. He says, " As I live, saith the Lord God, I have no pleasure in the death of the wicked; but that the wicked turn from his way and live. Turn ye, turn ye from your evil way for why will ye die ? " So it was with David; " Deliver me from blood-guiltiness, O God ! " Psalm li. 14. It was fear of blood-guiltiness that made David speak so plainly. So it was with Paul; he says, " I take you to record this day, that I am pure from the blood of all men," Acts xx. 26. So it is with ministers—we must acquit our conscience; and if you go to the judgment-seat unpardoned, unsaved, your blood will be on your own heads. As I was

walking in the fields yesterday, that thought came with overwhelming power into my mind, that every one I preached to would soon stand before the judgment-seat, and be sent either to heaven or hell. Therefore, brethren, I must warn you, I must tell you about hell.

III. Let us consider the names given to hell in the word of God. And the first is fire; it is taken from an earthly element suited to our capacity, as Christ takes to himself a name to suit us, as a shepherd, a door, a way, a rock, an apple tree, the Rose of Sharon, &c. So when God speaks of heaven, he calls it Paradise, a city which hath foundations, golden streets, pearly gates. Now, one of these names will not describe it, nor any of them; for eye hath not seen, nor ear heard; neither hath it entered into the heart of man to conceive the things God hath prepared for them that love him. So when God speaks of hell, he calls it " a furnace of fire," " a bottomless pit," " perdition." Now, one of these names will not do; but take them altogether, and you may conceive something of what hell is.

The first name given to hell is " fire." On the southern side of Mount Zion there is a valley covered over with vines; it is the valley of Hinnom where Manasseh made his children pass through the fire to Moloch. Now this is the name by which Christ calls it, " a valley of fire." And, again, he calls it " a furnace of fire," the walls will be fire, it will be fire above and below, and fire all round about. Again it is called a lake of fire. The idea is something like a furnace of fire; it will be enclosed with burning mountains of brass. There will be no breath of wind to pass over their faces; it will be flames of fire for ever and ever. It is called devouring fire. " Who among us shall dwell with the devouring fire." Isa. xxxiii. 14. Compare this with Hebrews xii. 29—" For our God is a consuming fire." It is the nature of fire to consume, so it is with the fire of hell; but it will never annihilate the damned. O ! it is a fire that will never be quenched; even the burning volcanoes will cease to burn, and that sun now shining sweetly upon us will cease to burn, and that very fire that is to burn up the elements will be quenched; but this fire is never quenched.

Another name given to hell in the Word of God is " the prison."

169

So we learn that the multitudes that perished at the flood are shut up in this prison. Ah! sinner, if you are shut up in it you will never come out till you have paid the uttermost farthing; and that you will never do—the bars are the justice and holiness of God.

Another name given to hell is, " the pit." Ah! it is the bottomless pit, where you will sink for ever and ever; it will be a continual sinking deeper and deeper every day. Ah! sinner, is it not time to begin and cry, " Deliver me out of the mire, and let me not sink ? " —" Let not the deep swallow me up, and let not the pit shut her mouth upon me ? "

Another name given to hell in the word of God is, " a falling into the hands of God." " It is a fearful thing to fall into the hands of the living God," Heb. x. 31. " Can thine heart endure, or can thine hands be strong in the days that I shall deal with thee ? " Ezek. xxii. 14. God will be your irreconcilable enemy, sinner. God, who takes no pleasure in the death of the sinner, but rather that he should live—that God, I say, will be your eternal enemy if you die Christless—if you will not believe—if you will not be saved. O! what will you do, poor sinner, when his wrath is kindled ?

Another name given to hell is, " the second death." " And death and hell were cast into the lake of fire. This is the second death," Rev. xx. 14. This is the meaning of God's threatening to Adam: " In the day that thou eatest thereof thou shalt surely die." Perhaps you may have stood by the bed of a dying sinner, and you may have seen how he gasps for breath—his teeth clenched—his hands clasp the bed-clothes—his breath turns fainter and fainter, till it dies away. Ah! this is the first death: and it is like the second death. Ah! the man would try to resist but he finds it is in vain; he finds eternal hell begun, and God dealing with him, and he sinks into gloom and dark despair. This is the death sinners are to die, and yet never die.

Another name given to hell is, " outer darkness." Christ calls it outer darkness. " But the children of the kingdom shall be cast out into outer darkness," Matt. viii. 12. " Bind him hand and foot, and take him away, and cast him into outer darkness." Matt. xxii. 13. You will see it also in 2 Peter ii. 4—" God spared not the angels that sinned, but cast them down to hell, and delivered them into chains of darkness." Again, Jude 13th verse—" Wandering stars, to whom is reserved the blackness of darkness for ever." O ! my dear friends, this is hell—" the blackness of darkness,"— " outer darkness "—" chains of darkness."

IV. I come now to show you that the hell spoken of in the Bible is not annihilation. Some people think, that though they are not saved, they will be annihilated. O ! it is a lie; I will show you that:

1. First of all, *by the cries of the damned.* " And he cried, and said father Abraham, have mercy upon me—for I am tormented in this flame," Luke xvi. 24. And again, look at the words in Matt. xxii. 12, " There shall be weeping and gnashing of teeth." O ! these plainly show us that it is no annihilation. In hell the multitudes will be bundled up together in the great harvest day. " Gather ye together first the tares, and bind them in bundles to burn them," Matt. xiii. 30. There will be bundles of swearers—bundles of Sabbath-breakers—bundles of drunkards—bundles of hypocrites— bundles of parents and children; they will be witnesses of each other's damnation.

2. Hell will be no annihilation, when we consider that *there will be different degrees of suffering.* " It shall be more tolerable for Tyre and Sidon at the day of judgment, than for you," Matt. xi. 22. And it is said, the Pharisees would receive " greater damnation." Every man is to be judged according to his works.

3. It will be no annihilation, if we consider *the fate of Judas.* " Woe unto that man by whom the Son of man is betrayed ! it had been good for that man if he had not been born," Matt. xxvi. 24. Judas is wishing he had never been born. I have no doubt he wishes to die, but will never be able to die. So it will be with all here who shall go to hell—all unworthy communicants. Ah ! I tell you, if you die Christless, you will wish you had never been born—you will wish you had never seen the green earth or the blue sky. Ah ! you will wish you had never been. O ! dear brethren, better never to have a being than to be in hell. Ah ! there are many in hell to-day who are cursing the day they were born.

4. It will be no annihilation, for *it is an eternal hell.* Some weak

171

and foolish men think and please their fancy with the thought that hell will burn out, and they will come to some place where they may bathe their weary souls. Ah! you try to make an agreement with hell; but if there ever come a time when the flame that torments your soul and body shall burn out, then Jesus would be a liar, for three times he repeats the words of our text, and says, it shall never be quenched. It is eternal, for it is spoken of in words never used but to denote eternity. " And the smoke of their torment ascendeth up for ever and ever," Rev. xiv. 11. Ah! you see it is for ever and ever. Again, " And the devil that deceiveth them was cast into the lake of fire and brimstone, where the beast and the false prophet are, and shall be tormented day and night for ever and ever," Rev. xx. 16. Compare this with Rev. iv. 9, 10, " And when those beasts gave glory and honour, and thanks to him that sat on the throne, who liveth for ever and ever," &c. So you see the torments of the damned are spoken of with the eternity of God. Ah! if ever there come a time when God ceases to live, then they may cease to suffer. Again, the eternity of hell and the eternity of heaven are spoken of in the very same language. " And there shall be no night there; and they need no candle, neither light of the sun; for the Lord God giveth them light: and they shall reign for ever and ever," Rev. xxii. 5. The same words that are used for the eternity of the saints, are used for the eternity of the damned. " They shall be tormented for ever and ever." O! sinner, if ever there come a time when the saints shall fall from their thrones, or the immortal crowns fall from their heads, then you may think to leave hell; but that will never, never be—it is an eternal hell, " for ever, and ever; " eternity will be never ending wrath, always wrath to come. O! that you were wise, that ye understood this, that ye would consider your latter end.

V. I intended to consider that this eternal hell is surrounded and closed in by the attributes of God, but I shall leave it, God willing, to another occasion. I shall now apply this:

First of all, *to you that are believers*. Dear brothers and sisters, all this hell that I have described is what you and I deserved. We were over the lake of fire, but it was from this that Jesus saved us; he was in the prison for you and me—he drank every drop out of

172

the cup of God's wrath for you and me—he died the just for the unjust. O! beloved, how should we prize, love, and adore Jesus for what he hath done for us. O! we will never, never know, till safe across Jordan, how our hell has been suffered for us—how our iniquity has been pardoned. But, O! beloved, think of hell. Have you no unconverted friends, who are treasuring up wrath against the day of wrath? O! have you no prayerless parent, no sister, nor brother? O! have you no compassion for them—no mercy's voice to warn them?

2. *To you that are seeking Christ anxiously.* I know some of you are. Dear soul, what a mercy in God to awaken you to flee from this fiery furnace! O! what a mercy to be awakened to flee—to be in earnest. Ah! your unconverted friends will tell you there is no need of being so anxious. O! is there no need to flee from the wrath to come? O! learn, dear soul, how precious Christ is; he is a hiding place from the wind, and a covert from the tempest. All the things in the world are like a speck of dust, all is loss for Jesus— he is all in all—he is free to you, beloved—take no rest till you can say, He is mine.

4. *To you that are unconverted.* Ah! you are fools, and you think you are wise; but O! I beseech you, search the Scriptures. Do not take my word about an eternal hell; it is the testimony of God, when he spoke about it. O! if it be true—if there be a furnace of fire— if there be a second death—if it is not an annihilation, but an eternal hell—O! is it reasonable to go on living in sin? You think you are wise—that you are no fanatic—that you are no hypocrite; but you will soon gnash your teeth in pain; it will come; and the bitterest thought will be, that you heard about hell, and yet rejected Christ. O! then, turn ye, turn ye, why will ye die?

Sabbath, July 15, 1842.

173

GOD'S RECTITUDE IN FUTURE PUNISHMENT

" Upon the wicked he shall rain snares, fire, and brimstone, and an horrible tempest: this shall be the portion of their cup, for the righteous Lord loveth righteousness."—Ps. xi. 6, 7.

PERHAPS some of you may remember, about six months ago I preached to you on the subject of an eternal hell—upon the worm that never dies, and the fire that is never quenched. There are many people that do not like to hear preaching about hell, and some people think that it is not preaching the gospel; nevertheless, it is the counsel of God.

There was one part of the subject which I had not time to enter upon, and for which reason I have chosen this text, and that was to prove that an eternal hell was consistent with all the attributes of God. " Upon the wicked he shall rain snares, fire, and brimstone, and an horrible tempest; this shall be the portion of their cup, *for* the righteous Lord loveth righteousness."

From this passage I draw these three propositions:

I. That hell will be sudden to the wicked. " Upon the wicked he shall rain snares, fire, and brimstone," &c.

II. That God will punish the wicked eternally because he loves righteousness.

III. I draw from this verse that God will justify the believer for the same reason that he condemns the wicked,—" For the righteous Lord loveth righteousness."

I. " Upon the wicked he shall rain snares, fire, and brimstone, and an horrible tempest; this shall be the portion of their cup." It is quite obvious that the description here given is taken from what befell Sodom, Gen. xix. 23–25. It was a fine summer morning, the sun had just risen and was shedding his rays down upon the meandering Jordan; the women were busy about their employment, the children were sporting in the morning sun, when suddenly darkness overcast the sky, and in a moment God rained fire and brimstone from heaven upon them. One moment they were rejoicing in the morning sun, the next they were weltering in the lake of fire. Brethren, I believe that for the most of these in this congregation who will finally perish, their destruction will be sudden. It is written, " Take heed to yourselves lest at any time your hearts be overcharged with surfeiting and drunkenness, and cares of this life, and so that day come upon you unawares." Observe these words— " And so that day come upon you unawares." Compare this with the words of the text. " Upon the wicked he shall rain snares." Both passages are taken from the way in which the fowler catches birds; he draws in the snare suddenly, else the bird would escape. Such is the way with the wicked; the second coming of Christ will be like a snare. And, brethren, I believe, again, it is so with all you who die without finding Christ, you will perish suddenly. " Upon the wicked he shall rain snares, fire, and brimstone, and an horrible tempest; this shall be the portion of their cup." There are many among you that do not believe that there is a hell. Though you read of it in the Bible, and are told about it, still you always put in a salvo to your conscience, perhaps there is not such a place after all—perhaps it is just a bit of priestcraft got up to frighten people with. I believe that many among you think that, and many of you will die thinking that; but, O, the moment you let go the last friend's hand that is grasping yours, that moment, sinner, when you find your soul in the presence of God, and when you find out for the first time that you have God to do with, that moment you will find that there is an eternal hell. " Upon the wicked he shall rain snares, fire, and brimstone, and an horrible tempest; this shall be the portion of their cup." O ! my brethren, methinks hell would not be so bad if you were counting the cost of it; but to have the eyes lifted on it in a moment, Ah ! you will know what the second death is then.

II. I come to the second proposition, and I desire your attention to it, for it is what I have chosen these words for. It is the righteousness of God which makes him punish the wicked eternally. Verses 6, 7, " Upon the wicked he shall rain snares, fire, and brimstone, and an horrible tempest; this shall be the portion of their cup, *for* the righteous Lord loveth righteousness." I believe there is a great deal of ignorance about an eternal hell. There are many men that think God will cast sinners into hell on account of mere passion. Now, it is right to know that God did not create hell merely out of passion. Brethren, if it was passion it would pass away. But it is not from mere passionateness that he has kindled hell. And it is right that you should still farther consider that it is not that God has pleasure in the pain of his creatures. I believe that God does not delight in the pain even of a worm. You will see this in Ezek. xviii. 23, " Have I any pleasure at all that the wicked should die ? saith the Lord God: and not that he should return from his ways, and live." And then verse 32, " For I have no pleasure in the death of him that dieth, saith the Lord God: wherefore turn yourselves, and live ye." You will observe in this chapter that you have it put in two forms; you have it put in the interrogative form, and then you have it in the affirmative. Again, we are told in the New Testament, that " God will have all men to repent, and come to the knowledge of the truth." " He is not willing that any should perish." And in the 17th chapter of Acts, it is said, " God commandeth all men every where to repent." These passages show that there is an essential benevolence in God, that he has no pleasure in the pain of his creatures. Speaking humanly, God would rather that the wicked should turn from his evil ways and live.

Some will ask, why then is there a hell ? The answer, brethren, and it is an answer I desire to be written on the heart, it is that the righteous Lord loveth righteousness. The only reason why God casts the unbelieving into the fire that never shall be quenched is, because God is a God of righteousness, and therefore he will reign till all his enemies are put under his feet. Perhaps brethren, some of you will say, why does his love of righteousness make him punish sinners in an eternal hell ? There are two answers to that: First, sin is an infinite evil, and therefore it demands an infinite punishment. I do not know if you understand this. The thing I was praying for in secret was, that I might be enabled to vindicate God's proceedings. Then, brethren, sin is an infinite evil, because it is the breaking of an infinite obligation. I suppose there are none here who will say

176

that God is not infinitely lovely; and therefore none will say that there is not an infinite obligation upon us to serve him. Then, if you and I do not this, we are breaking an infinite obligation; and if it be an infinite evil, then it demands infinite punishment. But how can man bear infinite punishment? If God were to put on infinite punishment who could bear it? Therefore it is eternal in duration,—"Upon the wicked he shall rain snares, fire, and brimstone, and an horrible tempest: this shall be the portion of their cup, for the righteous Lord loveth righteousness." I said there is another answer to the question; how is it a righteous thing in God to punish sinners eternally? You know you would not care what a criminal said at the bar whether his sentence was just or not. He might probably say it was not just; but you would believe the judge. Now, God says it is a righteous thing. "Seeing it is a righteous thing with God to recompense tribulation to them that trouble you." 2 Thess. i. 6. You will observe it is said, "It is a righteous thing." And how much more then will everlasting destruction be righteous. God's whole ways are equal. God who holds the balance in his hand, says it is a righteous thing. Dear brethren, I pray you in God's name to think of this. If punishment come from the righteousness of God, then there is no hope. If it were out of passion, then it might pass away. Often you observe a man whose face is red and swollen with passion, but it passed away. But ah! it is not out of passion. If it were out of passion surely God would have some pity when he saw the sufferings of the lost for many ages; but, ah! no. From what then does it proceed? It proceeds from the rectitude of God. If God can cease to love righteousness, then the fire may be quenched; but as long as he is a righteous God, that fire will never be quenched. Oh! brethren, it is a foolish hope you entertain that the fire will be quenched. I have seen some on their death-bed thinking that the fire may be quenched. Ah! it is a vain hope, sinner, God will never cease to be a righteous God. God will do anything to save a sinner; but he cannot part with his rectitude in order to save you. He parted with his Son in order that he might gain sinners, but he cannot part with his righteousness—he cannot part with his government; he would need to call good evil, and evil

177

good, first. "Upon the wicked he shall rain snares, fire, and brimstone, and an horrible tempest; this shall be the portion of their cup, for the righteous Lord loveth righteousness."

III. I come now to the last point, and that is that the very same rectitude saves the believer in Jesus, "For the righteous Lord loveth righteousness." I think this is the meaning of these words, "His countenance beholdeth the upright." The same thing is spoken of in the passage we read in Thessalonians, "It is a righteous thing with God to recompense tribulation to them that trouble you; and to you who are troubled rest with us," &c. The same thing we are taught in the 1st chapter of 1st John, 9th verse, "If we confess our sins, he is faithful and just to forgive us our sins, and to cleanse us from all unrighteousness." It is not said he is merciful, but he is just to forgive us our sins. The same thing we are taught in the 1st and 2nd verses of the 40th chap. of Isaiah, "Comfort ye, comfort ye my people, saith your God, speak ye comfortably unto Jerusalem, and cry unto her, that her warfare is accomplished, that her iniquity is pardoned; *for* she hath received of the Lord's hand double for all her sins." Here God puts the pardon of Israel on rectitude. "Her iniquity is pardoned: *for* she hath received of the Lord's hand double for all her sins." Why? because in her Surety she hath received double for all her sins. Suppose then you, a sinner, were to come to the Surety this night, you will observe that the sins you have committed are double paid. If the curse had fallen upon you, you could never have exhausted it; but when it fell upon the Surety, he exhausted it. And therefore upon the ground of equity, "she hath received of the Lord's hand double for all her sins." "He is just to forgive us our sins." — "His countenance beholdeth the upright."

My dear brethren, in impressing this subject upon you, I would speak.

1. *To those of you who are believers.* Dear brethren, you were once condemned to this hell. Over this hell you walked; but God has brought you to a Surety, where you have received of the Lord's hand double for all your sins. Prize this Surety. Ah! brethren, it is better to be saved through Christ, than even if it was possible

178

o be saved in any other way; for not only we are saved, but God's rectitude is displayed. Prize this Surety then.

2. I would say a word *to those of you who are under concern about your soul.* I am glad that there are any concerned. Oh! that I could say all were concerned. But, dear anxious friends, this is the hell you are going to by nature. I would say, then, see the necessity of fleeing from it. Many will say, there is no use of all that anxiety, if you need to fear, many will. But, dear anxious soul, if you have understood what I have been saying, you will see the necessity of a thousandfold more earnestness. Ah! it is a fearful hell; but, oh! it is more fearful to think that it is kindled by the rectitude of God. Ah! then there is need to flee. Dear, dear souls, do not be turned away by the world's flattery.

3. Let me speak *to those who are careless.* My dear brethren, I have showed you a solemn truth to-night; and unless I knew that no truth in itself will convert you, I might think that you would be converted by what you have heard. I have showed you that the destruction of the wicked will be sudden. Dear friends, do you think that it will be sudden? The very fact that you can sit so easily, shows that you do not believe it. Therefore when hell comes to you, it will come like a snare. Ah! dear, careless soul, think when you go home to-night, what if it should be to-night, "This night thy soul shall be required of thee." Careless sinner, what would become of you if God were to shoot his darts, and rain snares, fire, and brimstone upon you? Ah! tell me, sinner, would it not embitter your eternity to think that you were told of it? Ah! you are like Lot's sons-in-law, "he seemed as one that mocked unto them." Ah! do you think they thought it a dream when they lifted up their eyes in hell. And oh! sinner, will it not embitter your eternity to think you had been warned to flee? The minister is free of my blood. I was warned, but I heeded not. I am the cause of my own undoing; my hands have made the snare where-with I am caught.

Sabbath, Dec. 4, 1842.

THE VESSELS OF WRATH FITTED TO DESTRUCTION[1]

"What if God, willing to shew his wrath, and to make his power
known, endured with much longsuffering the vessels of wrath fitted
to destruction: and that he might make known the riches of his
glory on the vessels of mercy, which he had afore prepared unto
glory?"—ROM. ix. 22, 23.

IN a former discourse, brethren, I attempted to show you that the
reason why God will punish the wicked eternally is, because he
loveth righteousness. It is said in the eleventh Psalm, "Upon the
wicked he shall rain snares, fire, and brimstone, and an horrible
tempest: this shall be the portion of their cup, for the righteous
Lord loveth righteousness." I then tried to show you, that God has
created hell, and will maintain it for ever, not because he loves
human pain—I believe it is not so, nor is it because he is subject to
passion, as men speak of passion—but because the righteous Lord
loveth righteousness. And I showed you, as you will remember,
what a certainty hell is to the wicked. If it had its origin in the love
of human pain, then you might have hoped that it would have an
end; or, if it proceeded from passionateness, then it might cool;
but, ah! when it proceeds from Jehovah's love of righteousness, I
see, brethren, in that a reason why "the worm dieth not, and the
fire is not quenched." There is a second question which no doubt
has occurred to you: why are there any left unpardoned at all?
Why was Adam left to fall? Could not God have held him up? or,
if it was necessary that Adam should fall, in order that Christ might

[1] The following sermon preached on the afternoon of March 12, 1843,
was the author's last in St. Peter's. "It was observed, both then and on
other late occasions," says Andrew Bonar, "that he spoke with peculiar
strength upon the sovereignty of God." The following evening M'Cheyne's
illness commenced and on Saturday, March 25, he went to the Saviour
whose glory he lived to proclaim.

die, why are not all saved ? Surely there is efficacy in the blood of Christ to pardon all—why, then, are not all saved ? There are many answers to that question which we will know in a higher state of being; but here is one, " What if God, willing to show his wrath, and to make his power known, endured with much longsuffering the vessels of wrath fitted to destruction: and that he might make known the riches of his glory on the vessels of mercy, which he had afore prepared unto glory? " You will notice, brethren, that in these words the apostle Paul tries to give an answer to that question. He does not answer it directly, he employs a " what if."

Let us enter into this subject a little more deeply. There are three reasons set down here why men are allowed to perish.

I. The first is, *that God was willing to show his wrath*. These words are terrible. We are told frequently in the Bible of the wrath of God. It is not like human wrath: it is calm, settled—it consists principally in a regard to what is right. This is the wrath of God. We are told a great deal about it in the Bible. It is revealed against all sin. " For the wrath of God is revealed from heaven against all ungodliness and unrighteousness of men, who hold the truth in unrighteousness." Romans i. 18. Observe the word " all "—it is against *all* sin. Then Col. iii. 6, " For which things' sake the wrath of God cometh on the children of disobedience." We are told also, brethren, that this anger is constant. " God is angry with the wicked every day." Psa. vii. 11. The bow of God's justice is, as it were, already bent against the wicked, the arrow of God's justice is already on the string against the wicked. And then we are told that his wrath is *intolerable*. In the psalm which we were singing (Psa. xc. 11), it is said, " Who knows the power of thy wrath? " And we are told in Revelation, " The great day of his wrath is come, and who shall be able to stand? "

But we learn more by example than even by these declarations. We have many examples of God's wrath and its consequences. The first example we have is, *his casting the angels out of heaven.* We are told by Jude, " That the angels which kept not their first estate, he hath reserved in everlasting chains, under darkness, unto the judgment of the great day." And we are told by Peter, " That God spared not the angels that sinned, but cast them down to hell, and delivered them into chains of darkness, to be reserved unto judgment." Now, brethren, in several respects this was one of the greatest examples of divine wrath we have, for it seems to have happened in one day. One day these angels were in heaven—the next in hell. One day they were angels of light—the next fiends of darkness. And then this made it fearful, when the Lord left them no room for repentance. One thing the universe might have learned from this was, that God will *certainly* punish sin.

Another example of God's punishing sin was not in heaven, but on earth, when he sent the *deluge* upon it. "God saw that the wickedness of man was great in the earth, and that every imagination of the thoughts of his heart was only evil continually. And it repented the Lord that he had made man on the earth, and it grieved him at his heart. And the Lord said, I will destroy man, whom I have created, from the face of the earth." And so it came to pass: "The flood came, and carried them all away;" and it has left traces on our world still, to show that God will not fail to punish sin.

Another example of divine vengeance was, *when God destroyed Sodom.* "Now, the men of Sodom were wicked, and sinners before the Lord exceedingly." The cry of its wickedness went up to heaven, and God sent down two angels, to see if it was according to the cry that came up; and they found it even so; and, when they had taken out just Lot, God rained fire and brimstone upon the devoted city; and he has left traces of it there to this hour.

There was yet another exhibition of divine wrath on earth—*it was the death of God's dear Son.* If ever there was a time when God could have said that he would forego his wrath, it was surely this. It was this for two reasons. First, because the object of that wrath was dear to God. There never was one in the universe so dear to God as his Son. Another reason was, Christ had no sin of his own. Just as his robe was seamless, so was his soul sinless. Nay, brethren, that one act of his—laying down his life, was so glorious, as an exhibition of God's justice, that the universe never saw its "marrow." "Yet it pleased the Lord to bruise him." These words do not give

182

the least shadow of his suffering from God on account of our sin. Brethren, if any thing in the world can show that God will punish sin, it was the death of his dear and sinless Son.

There is one exhibition of his wrath yet to come. Verse 22— "What if God, willing to shew his wrath, and to make his power known, endured with much longsuffering the vessels of wrath fitted to destruction?" God is yet to destroy the souls that he has made—not the angels that fell, for he has done that already, when he cast them into hell, but the souls on which he has waited. There is to be a new exhibition of wrath that the world never saw the like of before. He is going to show what he will do to the despisers of his Son—to those who despise his gospel. It will be a new thing when "God will be revealed from heaven in flaming fire, taking vengeance on them that know him not, and that have not obeyed the gospel." God waits to show his wrath. Ah, brethren! it will be fearful to feel it—it is fearful even now to think of it. You know, when a vessel goes down at sea, it is customary to set up a beacon, to warn other vessels of the rocks that are there. So I believe it will be with the wicked: they will be beacons, to show how God will punish sin.

II. I come now to the second reason why any are left to perish—it is, *that God may show his power.* "What if God, willing to make his power known?" We are frequently told in the Bible of the power of God. He said to Abraham, "I am the Almighty God." We are told in the ninety-third Psalm, that "the Lord on high is mightier than the noise of many waters; yea, than the mighty waves of the sea." We are frequently told of his almighty power; and not only so, but we have brilliant examples of it. The first upon record is *creation.* "God said, Let there be light: and there was light." "He spake and it was done—he commanded and all things stood fast." Another example of the same thing is, the *constant providence* of God. "In him we live, and move, and have our being." He rides on the swift wings of the wind. Another example of the power of God is, *his restraining and bridling the wicked.* "Be ye not as the horse, or as the mule, which have no understanding, whose mouth must be held in with bit and bridle."—Ps. xxxii. 9. This is the way in which

God holds the wicked. Another way in which God makes his power known is, *in the conversion of souls*. "Not by might, nor by power, but by my Spirit, saith the Lord." This is said to be "the wisdom of God and the power of God." I believe the converting of a soul is something greater than the making of a world. Brethren, there is one exhibition of divine power that yet remains—it is, *the destruction of the wicked*. "What if God, willing to shew his wrath, and to make his power known, endured with much longsuffering the vessels of wrath fitted to destruction?" I believe, dear friends, that the reason why God has raised up Pharaohs is to show his power in them. He said to Pharaoh, "For this cause have I raised thee up, that I might show my power in thee." Now, I say, in regard of those of you in this congregation who will die unsaved, that God has raised you up, to show his power in you. Thus, it is said in Isaiah lxii., "I will tread them in mine anger, and trample them in my fury; and their blood shall be sprinkled upon my garments, and I will stain all my raiment." And then in Revelation xviii., "She shall be utterly burned with fire; for strong is the Lord God who judgeth her." And we are told by our Lord, in Matthew x. 28, to fear God, "who is able to destroy both soul and body in hell." You will notice in this passage that he says, "God is able to destroy"; and therefore, brethren, it is plain that there must be some great power exercised in his destroying the wicked; and I think it is to consist in this—*God will destroy their well-being, but not their being.* Here, then, is another exhibition of the power of God.

When lately in the north of Scotland, I stood on the sea-shore, and saw the rocks standing out of the sea. It was very remarkable to stand and see the mighty waves dashing upon the rocks. There were two things remarkable in it: first, the greatness of the rocks on which the waves dashed: second, the rocks remaining unmoved —no force of the waves could move them. Brethren, this scene is an emblem of what will be witnessed another day, when God shall pour out his wrath on the wicked. Ah, brethren! will it not be fearful to see God put out his power upon the wicked—to see him upholding them with one hand, and pouring out his wrath upon them with the other? Surely, brethren, the power of God's wrath is very great. If any of you have seen a great furnace, you will have seen the power that the fire has; but fire is God's creature. What must *his power be* who is the Creator ?

III. I come now to the third point—*the reason given why believers are saved.* Verse 23—" And that he might make known the riches of his glory on the vessels of mercy, which he had afore prepared unto glory." One reason why there are vessels of wrath fitted to destruction is, that God may show by contrast the riches of his grace on the vessels of mercy. You know, brethren, we learn many things best by contrast: for example, the rainbow is never seen so bright as in the bosom of a dark cloud. So, brethren, we shall never see the love and compassion of God in them that are saved so gloriously displayed as when we see his wrath poured out on the vessels of wrath. This, then, is one reason why there are vessels of wrath.

I believe that the " riches of glory " here spoken of are the whole rainbow of the divine attributes displayed in the salvation of souls. It was for this reason that God provided that there should be vessels of wrath fitted for destruction. This may appear to you very awful: it is so to myself. I could not and dare not speak of it if it were not here in God's own Word.

I would just show you one or two of his attributes that will be brilliantly illustrated in the salvation of souls. One is, *the sovereignty of God.* I have often told you of this. Many of you do not believe it; but there is a day coming when God will put it beyond a doubt. There are whole churches—whole bodies of professing Christians— that deny it; but there is a day coming when there will be none in heaven, or earth, or hell, that will deny it. Suppose that day were come, and this congregation divided, some on the left hand, some on the right, will you not see then God's sovereignty in the contrast ? You were once all the same. You were under the same condemnation. Some of you came out of the same womb—were nursed at the same mother's breast; yet it will be seen that some will be taken and some left. What made the difference ? Every creature will see that God made the difference, that he had " mercy on whom he would have mercy."

Another is, *the pardoning attribute of God.* At present this is

185

denied; but, brethren, in that day it will be made known. God will make known the riches of his glorious mercy on the vessels of mercy. O brethren, when one vessel is cleansed and taken up to glory, and another is left to perish, and when you see that they were equally sinful, then you will see that it was blood that made the difference. God will make known the riches of his mercy in the vessels of mercy, as well as his wrath in the vessels of wrath fitted to destruction.

Let us learn a few lessons from this subject. And—

1st. *All will not be saved.* It is a fearful delusion among you—I do not say you avow it, but you practically say, you believe—that there will be no hell. There are many of you that like to hear of *Hades*, and hope that it will turn out yet to be but a shadow. Brethren, there is a hell. It was God's plan that there should be vessels of wrath as well as vessels of mercy. Brethren, it is better it should be so. O do not dream! All will not be saved. There *are* vessels of wrath as well as vessels of mercy. Some of you, I think, are going to hell, and some, I trust, are going to heaven; and doubtless it is best it should be so, though I cannot explain the reason of it. The net has good and bad fishes: some will be taken into the vessel, and some will be cast away.

2nd. *Every one of you will be to the glory of God.* You will be made to glorify him in one way or another. You will either do it willingly or unwillingly. You *must* form a step to his throne. Ah, brethren! I believe each of you will yet be a beacon or a monument—either a beacon of wrath or a monument of mercy, "He hath made all things for himself; even the wicked for the day of evil." Yes, wicked man, you would rob God of his glory if you could, but you cannot. If you come to Christ, you will show forth his glory in saving you; but if you do not, God will show forth his power in destroying a vessel of his wrath.

3rd. There is a third lesson we may learn. It is, *the chief end of God in the world to manifest his glory.* Many think, especially infidel men, that God's chief end is the happiness of his creatures; but, from deep study of the Word of God for years, I see that it is not so. If that were his chief end, all would be happy. His chief end is

186

diverse—it is self-manifestation. Had it not been for this, God would have remained alone in awful solitude. I would desire to speak with deep reverence on such a subject. This seems to be the reason why there are vessels of wrath as well as of mercy—that they might be mirrors to reflect his attributes. And I believe, brethren, when creation is done, and when redemption is done, that there will then be a complete manifestation of the glory of God.

4th. Another lesson we may learn is, *God is longsuffering to the vessels of wrath.* I remember a person who once argued with me that she must needs be a child of God on account of his goodness to her. She enumerated many blessings she had received—how God had protected her in a foreign country, how many trials she had been delivered out of, and how many domestic comforts she had enjoyed. My only answer to her was, " The goodness of God leadeth thee to repentance." It is no proof that you are a child of God that God has borne long with you. There would be many children of God here, if this were the case. Ah, brethren ! strange though it may seem, he does not want *any* to perish—he does bear long with you.

Last of all, *the destruction of the vessels of wrath will be no grief to the vessels of mercy.* I once spoke to you of this before; but I would again remind you of it. The redeemed will have no tears to shed; and here is the reason—the very destruction of the wicked makes known the riches of divine grace. O my believing brethren, it will be an awful day when we shall not weep to see them perish. The day is hastening on—that day when no more rivers of waters will run down our eyes because they keep not God's law. But, O brethren, till that day come let us weep on; for, although God will be glorified in the destruction of the vessels of his wrath, he will be more glorified in making them vessels of mercy. The Lord bless his own Word. Amen.